THE CASE FOR THEOLOGY
IN LIBERAL PERSPECTIVE

Publisher's Note

THIS BOOK is one of a series of three, written at the request of the publisher: *The Case for Orthodox Theology*, by Edward John Carnell; *The Case for Theology in Liberal Perspective*, by L. Harold DeWolf; and *The Case for a New Reformation Theology*, by William Hordern. They are intended to provide for the lay person, student, teacher, and minister a clear statement of three contemporary theological viewpoints by convinced adherents to these positions.

Each author began with the same description of the purpose of the series and was provided perfect freedom to state his case. No one of the authors, moreover, knew the identity of the other two contributors until after manuscripts were completed; and at no time did any of the three have access to the manuscripts of the others.

THE CASE FOR
THEOLOGY
IN LIBERAL
PERSPECTIVE

by

L. Harold DeWolf

Philadelphia

THE WESTMINSTER PRESS

© W. L. JENKINS MCMLIX

LIBRARY OF CONGRESS CATALOG CARD No. 59–6062

PRINTED IN THE UNITED STATES OF AMERICA

To
Donald, Elaine, Daniel, and Edward

Contents

Acknowledgments

S O MANY PERSONS have contributed significantly to the Christian faith and the liberal perspective in which this volume is written that it is impossible to thank them. Were such acknowledgment to be made I should be required to speak not only of those who have purposefully encouraged me, but also of many who have challenged either my Christian faith or my liberal Christian heritage and so actually broadened the perspective in which I am impelled to think and write.

The section of Chapter I on natural theology includes much material from a paper originally presented to the American Theological Society, in April, 1958, and, in slightly revised form, published in the *Journal of Religious Thought*. Parts of that section were also included in a paper presented to the Methodist Theological Institute at Lincoln College, Oxford, in July, 1958. A smaller section of Chapter XI was first included in a paper presented to the Methodist Conference on the Theology of Christian Missions at Glen Lake, Michigan, in June, 1957, and later published in *Nexus*. I acknowledge gratefully the stimulation and instruction provided by criticism of these earlier efforts and the permission to draw on the published materials for these two passages in the present volume.

Quotations from the Bible are usually given in the words of the Revised Standard Version, by permission, for which I am grateful.

From several colleagues at Boston University School of Theology, especially Dean Walter G. Muelder, Professors Nils Ehrenstrom and S. Paul Schilling, and Librarian Jannette E. Newhall, I have received expert and valuable aid. Rev. John Howie has helped with proofreading and has done much of the work in preparing the index.

As always, I am deeply indebted to the faithful and discerning assistance of my wife, my constant helpmeet in the writing of books, as in all of life.

L. H. DeW.

9

Introduction

THE AUTHOR of the present volume is not a "liberal" in any meaning of that term as now most commonly understood in American theological circles. In the present fashion "liberal theology" is widely used as a whipping boy for all who condemn emptyheaded optimism, the substitution of current or past metaphysics for Christian faith, or a rational abstraction for a Christian understanding of man.

The current understanding of liberalism among theologians is less influenced by the actual methods and teachings of theological authors known to their contemporaries as liberals than by Reinhold Niebuhr's critical description of the movement. Niebuhr has rendered valuable service in exposing certain betrayals of the gospel in some popular preaching and teaching in liberal mood. Unfortunately, as Daniel Day Williams [1] and others have pointed out, Niebuhr often uses these distorted popular versions of liberal theology as typical of the whole movement. Many seminarians now practice tilting at these caricatures of liberalism and suppose that they are disposing of the methods and teachings of liberal theology for once and all.

This is a great pity. Niebuhr himself sees certain values in the liberal movement, values that he defends especially when arguing with Karl Barth and other European theologians. Both these values and others are in danger of being lost to a whole generation of Christians in America. Some preachers of a younger generation who never passed through the liberal struggle for intellectual freedom as

11

did Niebuhr, but who have been trained in the new antiliberal mood, are now preaching from our pulpits in ways increasingly difficult to distinguish from some of the older and more belligerent, narrow, and sterile types of fundamentalism. There is need to sound again the positive notes that were contributed by the older liberals at their best, and to show their relevance to the historic Christian faith.

This book, then, is written with a conscious concern for conserving certain values stressed by the outstanding Christian liberals. In that sense it is written " in liberal perspective."

However, I am not concerned, as I study the various problems of theology, with coming out at predetermined positions regarded as " liberal " conclusions. Few positions are so unenviable as that of the " liberal " who is determined at all costs to avoid traditional conclusions and is therefore condemned to illiberal and irrational partisanship. It is hard enough for a man to speak with approximate faithfulness the truth as God has given him to understand it, without being at the same time burdened with carrying the flag of this or that school of thought.

Much less am I concerned with defending the " liberalism " that Reinhold Niebuhr has attacked. He has characteristically defined that position in the following words:

> " The mystery of creation is resolved in the evolutionary concept. ' Some call it evolution and others call it God.' The Bible becomes a library, recording in many books the evolutionary ascent of man to God. Sin becomes the provisional inertia of impulses inherited from Neanderthal man against the wider purposes of mind. Christ is the symbol of history itself, as in Hegel. The relation of the Kingdom of God to the moral perplexities and ambiguities of history is resolved in utopia. The strict distinction between justice and love in Catholic thought is marvelously precise and shrewd, compared with the general identification of the *agapē* of the New Testament with the ' community-building capacities of human sympathy ' (Rauschenbusch). This reduction of the ethical meaning of the scandal of the cross, namely, sacrificial love, to the dimensions of simple mutuality imparts an air of sentimentality to all liberal Protestant social and political theories." [2]

When Williams asks what liberalism Niebuhr was describing here and points out that the description is not true of Hegel, Rauschenbusch,[3] Ritschl, D. C. Macintosh, Eugene W. Lyman, Robert Calhoun, or others whom Williams names, Niebuhr replies lamely that he was thinking of American liberalism and not European[4] (though he has named Hegel). He adds that he is "embarrassed" when Williams "names names," but he makes no effort to cite any such teachings from the Americans named or from any others. Probably the best that could be done to find support for his description in serious theological writing would be to cite one idea from one thinker and another idea from someone else and thus seek to construct the sort of synthetic doctrine he has described as liberalism. Even so, I doubt that the materials could be found in all the American liberal theologians together to provide for such a monstrous system of ideas. Much less does the account accurately describe the liberalism of any one important American theological writer who ever lived.

This book is not written to defend "liberalism." Yet I have felt obliged to write these few words to defend the memory of such faithful Christian theologians as Walter Rauschenbusch, Thomas Newton Clarke, William Adams Brown, Eugene W. Lyman, Albert C. Knudson, and many others. A thankless generation that distorts their teachings beyond recognition and then reviles the caricatures attributed to them is in danger of losing the intellectual freedom and integrity that their labors bequeathed to us.

Theologizing by the use of labels designating polemic stereotypes is especially unlikely to aid in the search for truth. Moreover, the dependence upon school labels, even when carefully designed, is perilous and sterile. Concerned, then, as I am, to restate and conserve some ideas emphasized by theologians often described by their contemporaries and sometimes by themselves as liberals, I am not concerned with trying to defend "liberal theology" or with trying to be a "good liberal."

However, there is another sense in which I find myself bound to study and write theology "in liberal perspective." The basic meaning of "liberal" is, of course, *free,* or, as Webster's Dictionary further puts it, "unrestricted." Any system of ideas is, in a sense, restricted, and certainly a Christian theology is restricted by being Christian and by being a theology. Yet Christian theology can be written in a *perspective* unbounded by presupposed limits. This is my intention.

Being written in liberal perspective, this work must take into account ecumenical Christian thought, without a decision beforehand to make every solution of a doctrinal problem come out with a traditional Reformed, Lutheran, or Methodist answer. Moreover, the perspective is even broader. In aim it is catholically human. The focus of attention is on the revelation of God to the Christian community. But no relevant consideration drawn from human experience is ruled out of bounds. To say in advance that Christian theology must consider only Biblical evidence or that it must take into account only the Bible, the creeds, and the church fathers — perhaps adding the Reformers — is too much like demanding that God must speak to me in the way I prescribe and in no other. To be sure, I must "test the spirits to see whether they are of God" (I John 4:1), but I must pay sufficient attention to any kind of voice or evidence that offers some prima-facie relevance to test it. Sometimes the intellectually as well as the humanely hospitable are surprised to find that they "have entertained angels unawares" (Heb. 13:2).

The reader may complain that this introduction leaves many questions unanswered, including many questions about method. I agree heartily. The book is not ending here; this is only the introduction! It is hoped that at least partial answers to some of these questions will be sought and, possibly, a few even found in the chapters that follow.

PART ONE
THE WORD OF GOD

I.

God's Communication to Man

ALL THEOLOGY REQUIRES BOTH REVELATION AND REASON

We know nothing about God that he has not chosen to communicate to us. Apart from him we know nothing, do nothing, are nothing. "It is he that made us, and not we ourselves." (Ps. 100:3, margin.) From conception through life we are constantly dependent upon him and the conditions that he provides for our existence, our growth, our knowledge, and our salvation.

Just now we are concerned with our knowledge that we have through the word of God. By the word of God, in the broadest sense, is here meant any act of God by which communication occurs between God and man. There is a narrower sense in which we may properly use the term "Word of God" to denote that great, cumulative series of divine acts to which witness is borne in the Bible. Strictly speaking, the Bible itself is not the pure Word of God. Although by a figure of intimate association we may, on occasion, without impropriety, call the Bible the Word of God, we ought not to use this language in careful theological discourse, for reasons to be observed later. There is a third and yet narrower sense in which God's communication to us in Jesus Christ, the Word become flesh and dwelling among us, is called the "Word of God." The narrower meanings, so richly concentrated with significance, will be employed in the two chapters following. In the present chapter the broadest significance is used. Here our attention is called to God's communication with man, however and whenever this may occur.

Every instance of communication requires two agents, one who speaks and one who hears, one who writes and one who reads, or one who acts and one who sees. The effectiveness of communication generally depends clearly on both the one who makes known and the one to whom something is made known. Deaf ears and blind eyes, as well as dumb lips and paralyzed hands, can bar communication. A poor television receiver, as well as a transmitter out of order, can produce a confused image.

In the case of divine-human communication, the one who receives is the creature of him who transmits the word. In that sense this communication is wholly dependent upon God. However, he has given to us some freedom to be open or closed to his word. Our attitude toward his word at one time affects our receptivity on later occasions. The receptivity of other men before us and beside us affects our own. Yet always, at every moment, our own decision affects the actual success or failure of the divine-human communication.

This two-sidedness of the divine-human communication has given rise to two sets of terms for describing it. When we think of the God who speaks the word, we call the event revelation. When attention is focused upon the man who hears, we speak of learning or discovery.[1]

Often a distinction has been made between *natural theology* and *revealed theology*. Natural theology is, then, that theology " which is based only on experience and reason." [2] The purpose of natural theology is " to set forth in a methodical, orderly way all that may be known concerning God and the world and man, and their mutual relations, from that general revelation which is given in nature, mind, and history." [3] As Lord Gifford specified in the provisions for the Gifford Lectures, natural theology must be developed " without reference to or reliance upon any supposed special exceptional or so-called miraculous revelation."

It is legitimate and useful to distinguish between natural theology and theology based upon the Biblical revelation. This is not, however, because natural theology is independent of revelation or because " revealed " theology is independent of human reason. Both are dependent upon God's communication to man. Such communication requires both God's revealing act and man's inquiring, discovering reason. The most spectacular, dramatic act of God communicates nothing to man, hence, achieves no revelation, unless it is perceived, understood, and accepted by a rational human being. On the other hand, the most inquisitive, sensitive, and clever human reason would never discover any truth about God if God did not so act upon man as to provide him with data to interpret.

Some recent theologians have denied the validity of natural theology, and many others have cast such doubt upon it that this subject requires our special attention.

THE VALIDITY AND USEFULNESS OF NATURAL THEOLOGY

By *natural theology* is here meant *the learning of some truth about God or about man's rightful destiny from considerations logically independent of the Biblical revelation and of a prior commitment to Christian faith.* For example, all five of Thomas Aquinas' famous philosophical arguments for God are exercises in natural theology. So also is F. R. Tennant's " wider teleological argument." [4] All ethical concepts of natural law, that is, moral law discoverable by philosophical method from broad considerations of reason and common human experience, are instances of natural theology.

Natural theology has a long and impressive history. It includes Socrates' belief in eternal unwritten laws; Plato's references to evidences of God's wisdom in the order of nature; Cicero's ridicule of the atheists' notion that a fortuitous " concourse of atoms " could have made this complex, meaningful world; the highly developed thought about God and moral law in the writings of Seneca; the ethics of Epictetus grounded in his belief in the controlling providence of God; Plutarch's doctrine of the goodness, perfect justice, and love of God, and also his firm belief in human immortality assured by the love of God.[5] Among Christians, too, many have used natural theology in approach to the Biblical doctrine, in communication with non-Christians, or in other ways. Among them are such figures as Justin Martyr, Clement of Alexandria, Origen, Athanasius, Gregory of Nyssa, Augustine, Anselm, Thomas Aquinas, Duns Scotus, Raymond of Sabunde, John Calvin, Richard Hooker, Hugo Grotius, the Cambridge Platonists of the seventeenth century,

Richard Baxter, John Locke, Joseph Butler, John Wesley, and many writers of more recent times.

Recently, however, the validity and usefulness of natural theology have been frequently challenged by influential Christian theologians. This negative attitude toward natural theology has raised one of the most conspicuous and important issues in current religious thought.

Sören Kierkegaard believed that the "infinite qualitative distinction" between time and eternity made quite impossible any crossing from man to God by the thought of man. Man can conjure up all kinds of human substitutes for God, but all of these are mere idols. The metaphysical task is for man simply impossible, as Socrates well knew. The only knowledge of God that is either possible for man or necessary to his salvation is the acceptance by faith of the supreme Paradox, the eternal God become man in time and crucified by men. This acceptance is not an act of the intellect, but is rather a passionate decision of the will. So runs Kierkegaard's thought.

Karl Barth professes to be "an avowed opponent of all natural theology," [6] because he is a Reformed theologian. Both "the Reformation and the teaching of the Reformation churches," he says, "stand in an antithesis to 'natural theology.'" [7] It is Barth's opposition to natural theology that is most consistent and influential in Christendom today. Moreover, his stated grounds for the rejection of natural theology include all those which are frequently encountered among the many theologians who wholly reject or radically minimize natural theology. These grounds now demand our careful attention.

A. *Grounds of Barth's Rejection*

1. Barth's Vocation as Reformed Theologian

When, in his Gifford Lectures, Barth disclaims any intention of making a direct contribution to natural theology, he recalls that he is a Reformed theologian and "it cannot really be the business of a Reformed theologian to raise so much as his little finger to support this undertaking in any positive way." [8] However, he concedes that some Reformed theologians have found no such incompatibility between their vocation and natural theology, [9] and even Luther and

Calvin made use of natural theology.[10] The incompatibility is not, then, self-evident, but must be explained.

2. *Sola Scriptura*

Barth holds that Luther and Calvin desired "to see both the church and human salvation founded on the Word of God *alone,* on God's *revelation in Jesus Christ,* as it is attested in the Scripture, and on faith in that Word."[11] Natural theology would build on something other than the Scriptures and God's revelation in Jesus Christ, hence, must be regarded as opposed to the basic principle of the Reformation.

3. *Sola Fide; Sola Gratia*

Similarly, Barth observes that natural theology assumes that some truth about God and rightful human destiny can be known independently of prior commitment to Christian faith and of the grace that God gives in and subsequent to such commitment. Natural theology therefore contradicts the Reformation principles *sola fide* and *sola gratia.* To attempt anything without faith and humble dependence upon God's grace is to perform an act of presumptuous, sinful pride.

4. *Natural Theology Leads Only to Idols*

The God who has made himself known to us in Christ, Barth contends, is not the "God" of Aristotle or of any other philosopher learning without benefit of the Biblical revelation.[12] Hence to worship the "God" of natural theology is only to worship the creature of man's reason, an idol of man's own making, an idol possessing no reality beyond man's deluded imagination. The one only God is not conceived in human thought at all. Thus, in his Gifford Lectures, Barth says concerning the Scottish Confession:

> "What is conceived by all other 'believers,' past, present, and future, whatever the manner, place, and date of their belief, is certainly not what the Scottish Confession means by the object of its profession. The Confession does not *conceive* its object at all, it *acknowledges* it: 'We confess and acknowledge.'"[13]

Similarly, in *Dogmatics in Outline,* Barth writes: "God is not only unprovable and unsearchable, but also *inconceivable.* No attempt is made in the Bible to define God — that is, to grasp God in our concepts." [14] To worship the " God " we conceive, on the other hand, is idolatry and anthropocentric presumption.

5. Total Depravity

Natural theology implies a denial of man's total depravity. Since man is known by the Christians to be totally depraved, able to contribute absolutely nothing to God's communication of himself, not even by some capacity or preparation to receive it, the whole notion of a natural theology is misconceived.[15]

B. *Evaluation of These Grounds*

1. If Reformed theology is true, then that is reason enough for not contradicting it, regardless of the calling to be a Reformed theologian. But why suppose that all which Luther and Calvin taught is true? Presumably they were men and not God. Some of Barth's strictures against idolatry might be brought against his own appeal to " the theology of the Reformation " as if this were for him final.[16] Moreover, when it suits his purpose, Barth does not, in fact, hesitate to depart from Luther and Calvin — for example, when he laments the fact that both of them made use of natural theology!

2. When Barth objects that natural theology is contrary to the Reformation principle *sola Scriptura,* it is quite proper to raise the question whether that Reformation principle is true. To assume that the authority of the original Reformation teachings is such that it must not be challenged would be, in fact, to contradict the principle that only the Scriptures have such authority.

Actually, however, neither of Barth's quasi-Biblical authorities, Luther and Calvin, taught that nothing could be known about God or about his will for men otherwise than through the Bible. It is interesting that Barth does not directly claim such doctrine to have been taught by the Reformers, although such a claim is implied by his argument. He says, rather, that " the revival of the gospel by Luther and Calvin consisted in their desire to see both the church and human salvation founded on the Word of God *alone,* on God's *revelation in Jesus Christ,* as it is attested in the Scripture, and on faith in that Word.[17] Is such a desire inconsistent with belief in the validity of natural theology? Certainly many kinds of knowledge and authority are valid on which it is not proposed to found the church and on which it is not supposed that human salvation is dependent.

It is obvious that Luther and Calvin were rightly concerned to deflate the presumptuous claims of the Roman Catholic Church for itself, its ever-accumulating traditions, its intricate system of doctrine and laws, and the authority of its priesthood. It is well-known that the Reformers were attacking these overweening Roman claims when they erected their principle, *sola Scriptura*. They were denying that the church had the right to demand of its members or its priests acceptance of doctrines additional to those taught or implied in the Scriptures. Both Luther and Calvin, but especially Luther, had, at times, sharply hostile things to say about philosophy. However, these antiphilosophical outbursts had only a historically accidental, and not logically essential, connection with the principle that the church should be founded solely on the Word of God, as attested in the Scriptures.

The example of both Luther and Calvin, as Barth regrets to observe, does include the positive use of natural law and, more guardedly, they affirmed signs of God in his natural creation. Such use of natural theology did not, as Barth supposes, contradict their principle *sola Scriptura,* for they did not hold that through such use of natural theology they had discovered new doctrines additional to the teachings of Scripture and necessary to salvation. Rather, they found in natural theology a confirmation of the Biblical teaching that God has provided all men with such a knowledge of him and of his will for them that they are without excuse for their sin and unbelief and are rightly under his condemnation.[18] Likewise Calvin found natural law, and even the laws enacted by magistrates, so long as consistent with God's commands, to be binding on the Christian conscience, while he insisted that no one had a right to "prescribe any new form for the worship of God, and impose a necessity in things that were left free and indifferent."[19]

It must be said further that if we were to maintain that the Christian ought to hold so exclusively to the Scripture as to deny the validity of any knowledge of God through other channels, then we should be contradicting ourselves. For the Bible itself occasionally refers to the teachings that God has given concerning himself through the world of nature (as in Job, chs. 37 to 41; Ps. 19:1-4; Matt. 5:44-45; Rom. 1:20) and concerning his righteous law in the natural endowment of the human heart (as in Rom. 2:1-2, 12-16).

3. The argument that it is proud and sinful to believe that any knowledge of God is possible prior to, or independent of, faith in Christ and with the aid of the grace imparted only to those who have such faith, requires careful attention.

Certainly this objection is not supported by Calvin's teaching. Calvin writes, "We lay it down as a position not to be controverted, that the human mind, even by natural instinct, possesses some sense of a Deity." [20] Even men's sin does not eradicate this knowledge of God, Calvin contends, though it does make it inoperative in the control of their passions. Thus he writes:

"Yet this is a further proof of what I now contend for, that an idea of God is naturally engraved on the hearts of men, since necessity extorts a confession of it, even from reprobates themselves. In the moment of tranquillity, they facetiously mock the divine being, and with loquacious impertinence derogate from his power. But if any despair oppress them, it stimulates them to seek him, and dictates concise prayers, which prove that they are not altogether ignorant of God, but that what ought to have appeared before had been suppressed by obstinacy." [21]

It is not proud and sinful to believe what is clearly the truth — a truth in this instance affirmed by Calvin and the Bible as well as by a great quantity of human experience. Calvin cited an exaggeration of this truth when he wrote, "Cicero observes, there is no nation so barbarous, no race so savage, as not to be firmly persuaded of the being of a God." [22] But that many peoples have possessed some ideas of God and strong beliefs in his existence without having so much as heard of Christ or the Bible is a truth incontrovertible by anyone open to persuasion by facts.

Actually, if we examine the natural theology of such men as

Cicero, Seneca, and Plotinus, to say nothing of Clement of Alexandria, Augustine, and Thomas Aquinas, we find a spirit much less proud and presumptuous than is displayed in the unsupported affirmations and denunciations of a Karl Barth which his sincere religious motivation does not excuse. The critical methods of philosophical study are employed, by the exponents of natural theology named, in the determination to escape substituting their own ideas for reality. This is an expression of humility, not of pride. It is not even pride in any proper special theological sense, for all the men named assumed a complete dependence upon God for all knowledge. Augustine and Thomas even acknowledged human depravity and constructed their natural theology with deference to this human disability.

To acknowledge the fact that many people possess some knowledge of God without any knowledge of Jesus Christ is not to say that they know him by their own resources, without assistance from God. The capacity for such knowledge may be regarded as a residue of the *imago Dei*, given by God's creative grace. On the other hand, it may be interpreted as a gift of his prevenient grace. It is interesting to observe that John Wesley subscribed sometimes to the one view and sometimes to the other.[23] Actually, if one regards all men as existing by the sustaining grace of God, then there is no such thing as a "natural" man without the grace of God. It is necessary to distinguish between men with and without that *saving* grace given to men of *faith*. At the same time, the question whether the knowledge possessed by men without faith is possessed "naturally" or by prevenient grace concerns a distinction with no ontological reference. There is no nature apart from grace.

4. One of the most serious examples of epistemological confusion in recent theology occurs in the argument that the "God" known to natural theology is only an idol having no ontological connection with the true God who has revealed himself to us in Christ. To support this notion two arguments are brought forth.

First, it is pointed out that the descriptions of him arrived at through natural theology are not identical with our knowledge of the Father of our Lord Jesus Christ. This is quite true, just as

Barth's writing about God is not identical — or consistent, in some details — with Augustine's or Luther's, or even as some of Barth's writing about God is not identical or consistent with other writing by the same author. Does this mean that Augustine, Luther, and Barth have written about different deities altogether, or that Barth has called us to the worship of as many idols as would correspond to his differing utterances about God less one? Not at all. It means that Augustine, Luther, and Barth have held differing conceptions of God, no one of which was identical with his very being, but all of which were by intention referring to him, whether accurately or erroneously. Ordinarily such distinctions are well understood. When some people speak of the president of the First National Bank in Centerville, others may speak of Mr. William A. Smith, and yet others of Daniel Smith's father. We do not insist that they are talking about different persons if we know that in fact Mr. William A. Smith *is* Daniel Smith's father and also president of the bank. Even if their characterizations vary greatly, we do not so insist. No more do differing accounts of the supreme Author and Ruler of the world imply various divine referents or one divine referent and a number of idols.

On the other hand, two accounts must have *something* in common if they are to be regarded as having the same objective referent. You and I may hear a noise at the door. I say it is only the wind, whereas you say there is a person knocking. A person and the wind are certainly not the same object. Yet we both are speaking of the one object, cause-of-noise-at-the-door, which we interpret very differently, at least one of us being in radical error. When is the referent the same, then, and when is it not?

Barth may insist that when, as Christian theologian, he speaks of God, he is speaking of God the Father of our Lord Jesus Christ. Since natural theology does not use that point of departure, its referent is not the same. Hence, despite the common use of the name God, natural theology and churchly theology are actually speaking of objects that are not to be ontologically identified. However, although using different points of departure and different ways of knowing, natural theology must often be speaking of the same God

who is the Father known through Jesus Christ, as is evidenced by
other signs of identification. Such signs are that he is the Author of
the world, our own Maker and Judge, or the Source of all good.
When Barth and the natural theologian are agreed that there is only
one such being, then it is plain that both are speaking of that one
same being. The further fact that the two accounts also differ in
certain respects does not disprove this identity, for as pointed out
earlier, our accounts of the same human person often differ sharply
In other words, there is much error mingled with our knowledge.
This is entirely true of our churchly theology as well as of natural
theology, as the conflicts and inconsistencies of churchly theologians
bear witness. It would hardly be either commendable or safe to
say that everyone with any mistaken ideas about God was an idolater! Who would be first to cast that stone?

Are there, then, no idols? We may properly call idols those objects of supreme human regard which are actually of man's own
making, not of his discovery through evidences that he has found.
Wealth or fame may be such an idol, as will also a carved object to
which a man does obeisance — if, indeed, the obeisance is done to
the artifact and not to God of whom the artifact may be a symbol.
When pagan peoples infer from natural phenomena or other evidences that there exist such numerous and unworthy deities as
Christians believe not to exist, these may better be referred to, as
they sometimes are in the Bible and in the early fathers, as false
gods, rather than as idols. Although figments of human imagination and in that sense man's creatures, their worshipers do not regard them as of their own making — as men do regard such idols as
wealth. Moreover, some beliefs about some deities of the polytheists
are of such character as to suggest that those who conceive and worship them must have been touched by the spirit of the one true God
and that these largely imaginary deities represent their earnest grop-
ings after a true understanding and worship of him whom we
know through Christ. To call all deities conceived by non-Christians
or discussed in natural theology " idols " is to lack the degree of discriminating discernment that befits both the man of understanding
and the humble man of God. Such rough and indiscriminate desig-

nation serves to express ill-concealed pride and to arouse attitudes of hostility, rather than to illuminate and clarify the distinctive character of the Christian knowledge of God.

Consider Brunner's statement:

> "He who believes that every revelation of God must say the same thing is preventing himself from understanding the Bible. It is the Triune God, it is true, who reveals himself in his works in the Creation and in the Law; but he does not yet reveal himself there *as* the Triune God. All church theologians, from the earliest days down to the present time, are agreed on this point. 'For there are two different ways of working of the Son of God; the one, which becomes visible in the architecture of the world and in the natural order; the other, by means of which ruined nature is renewed and restored.' " [24]

As a second argument, it is declared by Barth that every object of human conception is an idol,[25] while of the true God no conception is possible. Thus Barth writes:

> "God is not only unprovable and unsearchable, but also *inconceivable*. [German: *Gott ist nicht nur unbeweisbar und unerforschlich, sondern Gott ist auch unbegreiflich.*] No attempt is made in the Bible to define God, that is, to grasp God in our concepts [German: *Begriffen*]. In the Bible, God's name is named, not as philosophers do it, as the name of a timeless Being, surpassing the world, alien and supreme, but as the name of the living, acting, working Subject who makes himself known." [26]

In the latter part of this excerpt, Barth's argument again dwells on *differences* of conception, some of which, incidentally, misrepresent many of the philosophers. In the earlier part he is claiming that the Bible makes no attempt to present definitions or conceptions of God. This is patently false, as the examination of Isa. 40:18-29 will show. He seems also to suggest that we ought not to try to define what we mean by "God" or to represent him by concepts (German: *Begriffen*). Yet within four pages [27] he is defending the propriety of the "concept" (German: *Begriff*) "person," when properly understood, to represent each of God's "*three ways of being,*" and by page 44 he is pitying "the poor folk in the Eastern Church" who, he says, "have never quite understood the '*Spiritus, qui procedit a Patre Filioque.*'" Of course Barth can no more write about God without employing concepts than can any other author, Christian or pagan.

The proper objective is not to *avoid* concepts but to seek *accurate* concepts to represent faithfully the referent intended. When we are speaking of God we need to acknowledge humbly that the best of our concepts are bound to be extremely inadequate. Indeed, our best concepts are seriously inadequate to represent any concrete reality. Yet use concepts we must whenever we would speak concerning any object, even when the object is a personal subject, and even when the object is the Subject who is the Author of our being. The alternative to using concepts is an end of speaking (and writing) and likewise an end of discursive thought.

How much wiser was Calvin than Barth in this matter! When he writes about that knowledge of God claimed by Cicero for all nations and observable at times even in the most corrupt and blasphemous men, Calvin emphatically regards their knowledge as inadequate, as contradicted by their sinful actions and as requiring special revelation by the merciful God to be made effectual in governing their lives. But he grants that it is, nevertheless, knowledge of "God," the same God who judges them and who comes to us in Christ.[28]

5. Finally, the doctrine that man is totally depraved, in such fashion that he offers no capacity, need, or "point of contact" that can serve as a clue for natural theology, or even as object to which God addresses his revealing Word, is a gratuitous assumption. Even Calvin's doctrine of total depravity, extreme as it is, is a model of moderation and good sense by comparison. Barth purports to have drawn his doctrines from Paul's Letter to the Romans and from Reformed teaching. But the classical statement of Reformed doctrine on the specific issue at hand is given by Calvin, with explicit reference to Rom. 1:20, in the First Book of the *Institutes* (iii.1), as follows:

"We lay it down as a position not to be controverted, that the human mind, even by natural instinct, possesses some sense of a Deity. For that no man might shelter himself under the pretext of ignorance, God hath given to all some apprehension of his existence, the memory of which he frequently and insensibly renews; so that, as men universally know that there is a God, and that he is their Maker, they must be condemned by their own testimony, for not having worshiped him and consecrated their lives to his service."

This statement of Calvin's does not throw light on that other problem, What is the status of religious pagans who *do* worship God and *do* consecrate their lives to his service? Paul does at least suggest an answer as he writes in his Letter to the Romans:

"When Gentiles who have not the law do by nature what the law requires, they are a law to themselves, even though they do not have the law. They show that what the law requires is written on their hearts, while their conscience also bears witness and their conflicting thoughts accuse or perhaps excuse them on that day when, according to my gospel, God judges the secrets of men by Christ Jesus." (Ch. 2:14-16.)

Yet, while Calvin may hesitate to go all the way with Paul, he nevertheless is clear as to man's capacity (or "natural instinct") to know that God is his Maker.

There is here no question regarding the powers of man alone. "Man alone" is a fiction especially absurd in the discussions of theologians who believe that man exists by the grace of God and is always in his presence. Of course "man alone" cannot construct a natural theology, since "man alone" cannot even exist. On the other hand, man as he is, empowered by the grace of God and surrounded by evidences of "his eternal power and deity" (ch. 1:20), plainly can and does construct natural theologies true as far as they go. To say that this is impossible is an unwarranted assumption, opposed by the facts of human history, the teaching of the Old and New Testaments, and the testimony of that very Reformed tradition to which Barth professes commitment.

C. Positive Usefulness of Natural Theology to the Christian Theologian

In defending his right to give the Gifford Lectures, despite his rejection of all natural theology, Barth makes the claim that natural theology soon becomes "arid and listless" when it is not in "conflict" with its "adversary" which stands in "clear antithesis" to it, namely, "the teaching of the Reformation." [29] He says this dependence of natural theology on opposition by a revealed theology that absolutely rejects it is "notorious," [30] but he does not cite a shred of evidence. Actually, the natural theology of the Stoics was ably constructed without such opposition and still retains sufficient vitality to exert considerable influence on the law and on international affairs as well as on philosophical and theological theory, especially through its concept of natural law. The natural theology of Thomas Aquinas and of many writers in the seventeenth, eighteenth, and nineteenth centuries flourished with the encouragement, rather than with the opposition, of most theologians with whom these writers were much concerned.

That natural theology is radically inadequate soil for the nurture of a living, redemptive faith would be cheerfully admitted, or rather emphatically asserted, by most of its Christian participants. But it is quite another thing to say that natural theology owes its vitality to opposition by theologians who attack it. This latter proposition is not only unsupported by the evidence but is disproved by the history of natural theology.

On the other hand, Christian theology needs the services of natural theology for several purposes. These can be given only brief statement here.

1. A part of the total task of Christian theology is to determine the kind of relations that subsist between Christian doctrines and all else that we know. The fulfillment of this purpose requires inevitably that questions of natural theology be raised, such as these: What evidences of God's existence and of his nature are to be found in the world? In what ways does man's need of God appear in human nature? A Christian theology that does not include the con-

fronting of such questions has not yet taken seriously the effort to attain that wholeness of view required by the commandment to love God with all the mind. Barth, too, takes such questions seriously, but he argues that the answers to them would be wholly negative. The point is that such questions must be earnestly confronted, and if some positive lines of evidence are found to lead from man and the world to God, it is an obligation of the Christian theologian to explore these connections with care.

2. Natural theology serves to correct some of the errors produced by an exclusively Biblical or by Biblical and traditional theology. For example, Calvin was assisted by the natural theology of Cicero and others toward giving due emphasis to the first two chapters of Romans and putting in proper perspective Paul's other teachings, stressing our dependence on revelation and divine grace. On the other hand, Barth's own theology has in other ways obviously gained considerably over Calvin's by more recent developments based on presuppositions of natural theology. For example, Barth is not bound by any such rigid doctrine of Biblical inerrancy as restricted Calvin. This, of course, is due to the advances of textual and historical criticism. Barth takes these critical studies into account only spasmodically, yet they have given his use of the Bible much more flexibility than Calvin knew. But textual and historical criticism grew out of altogether secular literary and historical scholarship and are based on the assumption that there is continuity between the Biblical revelation and the rest of human history. Every time we use historical criticism in our study of the Bible, we are learning something about God's Word to man from historical knowledge gained from sources independent of the Biblical revelation. Biblical theology that makes use of historical criticism, then, implies the positive usefulness of natural theology.

To use another example, we may point out that the thought of the church has been stimulated, challenged, and modified for good, in recent times, by secular movements of thought. Reinhold Niebuhr, John C. Bennett, Walter G. Muelder, and other students of Christian social ethics have often pointed out examples of such contributions from non-Christian and even anti-Christian thought. To recognize such contributions is to imply acknowledgment of indebtedness to natural theology, for natural theology is the gaining of " truth about God or about man's rightful destiny from considerations logically independent of the Biblical revelation and of a prior commitment to the Christian faith." [31]

3. Natural theology provides a bridge for communication and intellectual co-operation of Christian theology with the natural and social sciences. Where Christian theology is taught as part of a university curriculum, it can scarcely participate in the common intellectual life of the university without accepting the services of natural theology. A department of Christian theology in which natural theology is opposed can issue pronouncements, and its members can as individuals participate in scientific activities. But can it participate in co-operative truth-seeking efforts with the sciences? Universities and our whole culture are already suffering badly from the disunity of intellectual fragmentation. Christian theology can be of important assistance in healing this condition, but only when it approaches other disciplines with a willingness to learn from them concerning its own subject matter, as well as to teach them important insights concerning their subject matter. To engage in this kind of co-operative intellectual task, with psychology, sociology, history, medical science, economics, political science, biology, and the physical sciences is to accept the services of natural theology.

4. In some aspects of human life, if the practical as well as the intellectual purposes of Christian theology are to be achieved, its participants must engage in certain common tasks with persons who stand outside the Christian faith. A common platform for such co-operation, for example, in the United Nations and its affiliated agencies is to be found in that division of natural theology concerned with natural law. The work of such men as Dr. Frederick Nolde suggests what can be done by men with Christian faith clarified by theological study and with willingness to enter wholeheartedly into discussion of current international issues on the basis of a humanly discoverable natural law. A Christian theology that includes the conviction that all natural theology must be rejected is cut off from effective participation in such important Christian ministries of conciliation and understanding.

5. In the communication of Christian faith — and Christian the-

ology — to unbelievers, natural theology is so valuable as to be well-nigh indispensable. While studying and otherwise assisting theological education in Central and East Africa, in 1955-1956, the writer asked many articulate first-generation Christians what had motivated their turning from paganism to Christian faith. Invariably, an important part of the answer implied the truth of natural theology. These young Christians told me that the Christian message showed them clearly what they had long dimly understood — the kind of life they ought to live, with faith in the one supreme God. The Christian faith declared to them the God already dimly sensed but yet not well known, and enabled them to live a life in fulfillment of moral needs long felt but inarticulate and ineffectual. In evangelistic approach to communists in the United States, I have found a similar necessity to meet the unbeliever on a common ground of secular thought and universal human need. Philosophical criticism of Marxism and a positive arguing of natural theology must be used until the unbeliever is persuaded that it is reasonable to look for a solution of his most perplexing theoretical and practical problems in a theistic faith. Until he is so persuaded, all citations of Biblical and churchly authority only confirm him in his assurance that the Christian faith is an outmoded, prescientific superstition. Natural theology is no less valuable for the evangelistic Christian world mission today than when Justin Martyr wrote his apology or when Augustine was led through Platonism to Christ.

So valuable an ally deserves a better reputation with Christian theologians than Barth and some others would give it, unless better reasons can be adduced against it than have thus far come to light.

It is encouraging that in his later writing Barth has come nearer to conceptions of natural law by his doctrine of the "spheres and relations" (*Bereiche und Verhältnisse*) in which he says God as Creator has placed man to live "dutifully or undutifully" (*gehorsam oder ungehorsam*).[32] Moreover, Barth has learned to say that what God has commanded us in Christ is required of all men, and that the revealing work of Christ is not limited to those who have been reached by the church or by knowledge of the historical Jesus. In places such doctrines seem to bring Barth close to a teaching practically equivalent to doctrines of natural law and of natural theology, under other names and with dialectical modifications.[33] However, such devious, subtle, and ambiguous expressions will not adequately counteract the influences set loose in theological thought by his earlier direct, clear, and sustained attacks on natural theology.

In many colleges and universities throughout the world various philosophies confront each other in vigorous opposition. Some teachers of philosophy interpret human experience in the terms of Marxian dialectical materialism. Some contend for other naturalistic philosophies without God. Others maintain that even to suggest that a divine purpose and power undergird this universe is to raise a nonsensical question. Countless students guided by such teachers of philosophy are convinced by them and so turn sadly from the church and from all consideration of the Christian faith. If there is no God, as their teachers have convinced them there is not, then obviously the Bible is simply false and its teachings outworn superstitions unworthy of serious consideration by honest and intelligent people.

At the same time, in other classrooms other philosophers are teaching that the world of nature and human nature cannot be explained in material terms and yet demands more unified and deeply meaningful explanation than the special sciences alone can give. Many of these philosophers proclaim the evidences of reason and purpose underlying the whole universe and so point their students toward God. In such classrooms Christian students find collateral confirmation of their Christian faith, and non-Christian students often begin thinking that religion may be, after all, a live option for honest people of the twentieth century. Some such students then turn to the church, listening eagerly to the gospel of Jesus Christ.

Such philosophical debates have been going on for many centuries. The incredible tragedy is that in our time many theologians have allied themselves with the philosophical foes of belief in God and hence of the Christian faith. Denouncing all philosophical approaches to God as idolatrous and presumptuous, they declare that man's reason is so corrupt that to our best thought, and hence to the best philosophy of which men are capable, atheism is the stronger contender. Nature and human nature, they say, appear to human reason as the mere products of blind force or chance, or else they say that the very questions about God are nonsensical until one has already accepted Jesus Christ by faith.

In short, the current theologians who renounce the possibility of natural theology are giving comfort to the deadliest enemies of the Christian faith to be found in the world today. These same theological foes of natural theology are deliberately undermining the prestige and increasing the difficulties of the best friends of the church and the Christian faith in the field of philosophy. The Christian philosopher finds himself confronted by able and dangerous contenders against all belief in God. While he wages this intellectual battle he now finds himself continually sniped at from behind by Christian theologians who would surrender on this field of battle at once, hoping to win on the church's home ground where the gospel is simply proclaimed, without argument for its truth. Unfortunately, most of the students who have, in the halls of philosophy, acknowledged the defeat of their belief in God consider that it would be dishonest for them now to take seriously the Christian proclamation. Consequently they will not be in church to hear it. The few who are will, for the most part, regard the whole teaching of the church as a nostalgic remnant of prescientific superstition.

All this is quite needless. Such men as Frederick R. Tennant, Edgar S. Brightman, William Ernest Hocking, Charles Hartshorne, and Peter A. Bertocci have demonstrated and are demonstrating that a philosophy pointing to God need ask no quarter in the great debate with philosophical atheism. In the minds of innumerable men and women such able philosophers are winning the debate and sending into the church eager listeners to the full gospel of Christ. The sad fact is that in this magnificent service to truth and to God they must fight against so many theologians, with their denunciations of the presumptuous pride of natural theology and their insistence that the Christian proclamation is in discontinuity with all that men rationally know or believe from other evidence.

" Test the Spirits "

Whether we are concerned with God's Word to us in the order of his visible creation or in our own human nature or in the series of historical events interpreted in the Bible or in our present religious experience, discrimination is needed. Many contrary voices and interpretations crowd upon us. We cannot accept all as authentic revelation. " Beloved," we read in The First Letter of John, " do not believe every spirit, but test the spirits to see whether they are of God." (I John 4:1.)

Unfortunately, it is not so easy to " test the spirits " as we might think. Many voices in our day can easily pass the test prescribed in I John, if understood literally, and yet conflict violently with one another and with Christ. There is many a voice " which confesses that Jesus Christ has come in the flesh " (I John 4:2) but which teaches hate rather than Christian love, or which speaks in tones of strident arrogance rather than of reverent humility. Those who would deny Christ may now begin by lip service to orthodoxy.

A church superintendent visited a theological school for a day and preached in the chapel. His sermon was a plea for the maintenance of a very " high " Christology. Again and again he insisted that Jesus was God and must be acknowledged as the all-wise, omnipotent God himself. After his sermon he invited students approaching graduation to meet him and discuss the possibility of accepting pastorates in his district. In support of his invitation, he expressed the belief that in his district a young minister could start with a higher salary, in more pleasant surroundings, and with prospects of more rapid advancement than anywhere else in America. Later he complained that not one student went to see him. Perhaps if he had heard some student conversations after chapel, he would have understood the reason. In one group a student asked, " What did you think of the Christology? " Another replied: " Which one? The one preached in the sermon or the one implied in the invitation to his district? "

Precisely! It is one thing to say in words that " Jesus Christ has come in the flesh." It is another to act in obedience to him. If a voice proclaims in words that Jesus is Lord but summons us to self-seeking privilege, it is plain that the call is not honoring the Christ who gave himself on the cross and who bade every disciple " deny himself and take up his cross and follow me " (Matt. 16:24).

The first test, then, for the Christian, is harmony with the spirit of Christ. Christians have found that Christ, the Word made flesh, gives new meaning to life. In him things hang together and make sense. Not only in theory but in life itself our faith in him releases the tangled threads of our experience and weaves a pattern of truth and self-fulfillment. We find him to be "the way, and the truth, and the life" (John 14:6). Whatever conflicts with him opposes the whole matchless harmony and integrity of the life that is centered in him. Such discordant ideas or enticements must therefore be resisted as falsehoods and temptations.

Any voice that claims to speak a word from God must also meet other relevant tests of experience. What is plainly contrary to the tested results of historical study or the physical sciences is to be regarded with some skepticism. It is true that some ideas believed to be thoroughly established are later proved false. However, as between a large body of systematized information such as we have in a highly developed science and a single contrary claim, the probabilities are that the science is more nearly right. When I am told of "revelations" that the sun circles a stationary earth, that no species of living things has evolved from another, or that there is no sin, sickness, or death, the revelation claim is found wanting in the test of experience.

In such testing there is always a possibility of my being mistaken. However, it is quite impossible to accept all contrary truth claims at face value, and I am responsible for discriminating to the best of my ability between truth and falsehood. To be careless and easy-going in the acceptance of every claimant as the voice of God is to be a willing idolater as well as a fool.

But what shall we say of those instances in which the evidence seems incoherent? Reinhold Niebuhr raises this issue in his essay "Coherence, Incoherence, and the Christian Faith." [34]

Niebuhr begins by observing that "the whole of reality is characterized by a basic coherence. Things and events are in a vast web of relationships and are known through their relations." [35] Yet, he observes,

> "There are configurations and structures which stand athwart every rationally conceived system of meaning and cannot be ap-

preciated in terms of the alternative efforts to bring the structure completely into one system or the other." [36]

How does one know that these obstructing "configurations and structures" are real? Obviously because without them some data of our experience are inexplicable. In short, we know them because they give coherence to certain portions of our experience. Do they at the same time make impossible a more inclusive coherent account? Assuredly they may often make quite inacceptable any *simple* scheme that, abstractly considered, might look attractively neat and tidy. But do they literally "stand athwart every rationally conceived system of meaning"? If "rationally conceived" means abstractly conceived, without reference to experience, undoubtedly they do. But no serious philosopher of our times would contend for any such conception. Niebuhr's favorite illustration is instructive and he introduces it right at this point:

> "The primary example is man himself, who is both in nature and above nature and who has been alternately misunderstood by naturalistic and idealistic philosophies. Idealism understands his freedom as mind but not his reality as contingent object in nature. It elaborates a history of man as if it were a history of mind, without dealing adequately with man as determined by geography and climate, by interest and passion. Naturalism, on the other hand, tells the history of human culture as if it were a mere variant of natural history." [37]

As I read such passages I wonder *what* idealism Niebuhr has in mind. Such different idealists as Hegel, Josiah Royce, William Ernest Hocking, and Edgar S. Brightman come to mind. Of none would Niebuhr's statement be true. Consider, for example, these words of Brightman:

> "Freedom of will does not mean complete self-determination, without regard to past experience or the rest of the universe; it means, rather, the power to choose from among the given possibilities. The possibilities are determined by the past history and the present environment of the individual." [38]

On the other hand, many naturalists recognize much more of man's freedom and responsibility than Niebuhr acknowledges.

In short, any philosopher worth his salt knows that man is not such a simple being as Niebuhr represents the opposing philosophies as presenting. However, all accounts, including Niebuhr's, doubtless leave unresolved problems. The complete understanding of man and his situation has been revealed neither to philosopher nor to theologian.

Some of the most searching insights into man's nature and predicament are provided by such Biblical accounts as Niebuhr calls "suprarational affirmations of the Christian faith." [39] In what sense are these affirmations "suprarational"? Certainly they are not learned by deductive logic. But are they beyond discursive exposition and critical rational evaluation? By no means. The present writer can wholeheartedly applaud Niebuhr as he says,

> "The question to be considered is in what way these suprarational affirmations are related to and validated by their capacity to resolve and clarify the antinomies, the aspects of uniqueness and particularity, the obscure meanings and tangents of meaning in human life and history." [40]

Exactly. In other words, they are to be tested by the criterion known in philosophy as empirical coherence. How strange, then, is Niebuhr's next sentence:

> "Judged by any standard of coherence and compared with other high religions, Christianity seems to be a primitive religion because all of these are more, rather than less, rigorous than science and philosophy in their effort to present the world and life as a unified whole and to regard all discords and incongruities as provisional or illusory." [41]

More rigorous in abstract unity, yes; but less rigorous in faithfulness to the empirical data than either science, sound philosophy, or true Christian faith! Less empirical, hence less coherent with the facts of our human experience!

If this same criterion of coherence, this "capacity to resolve and clarify the antinomies, the aspects of uniqueness and particularity, the obscure meanings and tangents of meanings in human life and history," were to be applied throughout our testing of revelation claims, we should be properly combining rational inquiry with faith in revelation. By such means we must " test the spirits to see whether they are of God."

FAITH AND REASON

When the evidence indicates where truth lies, then the reasonable man commits himself to that truth. We are not asked to believe recklessly, without evidence. Where belief without reason is demanded, every irrational cult, political delusion, and stupid superstition has the same claim to our confidence as Christian doctrine.

To be sure, there is a sense in which our commitments always go beyond the evidence. Our reasoning from evidence can never establish theoretical certainty about anything but abstract analyses. In the physical and social sciences, in philosophy and in the practical affairs of life, we can rationally establish relative probabilities, but no more. When we make decisions to submit to surgery, to marry, or even to eat the food before us, we act decisively, although the evidence that supports our assurance is always in some respects indecisive. The decisiveness of practical faith is a leap beyond the relative probability of evidence.

However, when people urge the " leap of faith " they sometimes mean something radically different from this. Some things that they believe, they say, can be proved. Others they believe without a shred of evidence, simply by a " leap of faith." In many instances such reports do not do justice to the actuality. There are often evidential connections of important significance which are discerned and on which faith is established, but which are not recognized as rational considerations because of preconceived narrow ideas of rationality. For example, a man may have found that many ideas he has learned from the New Testament have given to his experience new coherence and rich meaningfulness. He therefore develops high respect for the authority of the New Testament and accepts " on faith " other ideas found there. This is, of course, a rational extension of belief, whether or not adequately justified in a given instance. On the other hand, if a man literally believes with no reason to believe, he is being recklessly irresponsible.

The New Testament is full of arguments in support of the belief that Jesus is the Christ, rightful Lord of life.

As the first great missionary, Paul, went from place to place, he made it his regular method to argue the case for Christian belief. Usually, in a new community, his work centered on a Jewish synagogue. He therefore began with the beliefs shared by Christians, Jews, and the Gentiles who had accepted much of Jewish teaching ("the devout"), and from the Old Testament he sought to prove that Jesus was the long-awaited Messiah. The pattern is well described as follows:

> "Paul went in, as was his custom, and for three weeks he argued with them from the scriptures, explaining and proving that it was necessary for the Christ to suffer and to rise from the dead, and saying, 'This Jesus, whom I proclaim to you, is the Christ.'"
> (Acts 17:2-3.)

When Paul was approaching people who had not this common background of belief in the Old Testament, he confronted a harder task. However, he did as everyone must who seeks to persuade by reason. He found common ground with his audience and built his argument upon that basis. Thus in Athens he made his usual approach through the synagogue (Acts 17:17) but also approached the Athenians and foreigners frequenting the market place where Socrates had taught four and a half centuries earlier. In addressing these men he began with their acknowledgment that there might be a god unknown to them, moved from that to a general belief in the divine Creator, quoted a Stoic philosopher-poet's testimony to God, and went on to proclaim Jesus Christ as "a man whom he has appointed." (Vs. 22-31.) He was remarkably successful, too, as he made this apparently unplanned Athenian campaign. (Vs. 15-16.) To be sure, some scoffed and some procrastinated, but "some men joined him and believed, among them Dionysius the Areopagite and a woman named Damaris and others with them" (v. 34).

The Gospels are themselves obviously intended to give evidence of Christian claims. The genealogies of Matthew and Luke were clearly meant to show Jesus' Davidic lineage, and the accounts of his kindness, wisdom, courage, and miracles were well calculated to win the minds and hearts of readers. (Cf. Matt. 11:2-5.) All the Gospel writers could well write as did the author of the Fourth Gospel:

"Now Jesus did many other signs in the presence of the disciples, which are not written in this book; but these are written that you may believe that Jesus is the Christ, the Son of God, and that believing you may have life in his name." (John 20:30-31.)

The fact that we live in an age in which miracle stories are a stumbling block rather than an evidence of truth does not change the importance of the rational appeal that such accounts once made to people whose presuppositions led them to expect such signs of divine authority. The mood and thought of our age, however, require that the gospel be communicated in terms intelligible and persuasive to twentieth-century minds. To declare the Christian faith today only in terms of Biblical language and argument would be as foolish as Paul's method would have been had he approached the Athenian synagogue with quotations from the Stoics or started his address in the Athenian market place with Old Testament prophecies.

The insistence of some conservative Christians on a Biblical literalism that is rationally indefensible and an appeal based on the " proofs " of prophecy and miracles, in defiance of the natural sciences and the new historical understanding of Biblical times, needlessly drives from the Christian faith intelligent young people who will not blind themselves to scientific and historical evidences. If to be a Christian requires them to begin by being intellectually dishonest, they want none of it.

There is another way, too, in which conservative Biblicism does inestimably great damage among present-day adults and the youth of our high schools and colleges. That is by giving the impression that Christian faith is essentially unreasoning dogmatism that could not stand the light of candid examination. This impression is conveyed by emotional denunciation of all views opposed to the speaker's beliefs, by the condemnation of well-established scientific theory, and by warnings against the " sin " of doubt. Often critical, honest questions are met by such warnings rather than by attempts to give candid answers. It is slight cause for wonder that many inquiring youth who meet such tactics decide that their Christian ministers and teachers do not believe that their own teachings could bear the light of honest study. The writer has encountered, in universities and among adult acquaintances, many persons who, as a result of such experiences, have sadly forsaken the faith in which they had been reared and subsequently lived in barren faithlessness. The ease with which many such persons can be led into a mature, intelligent, and deeply consecrated Christian life, when a few candid discussions of their intellectual problems have removed the obstacles of doubt, shows how needless and tragic is the damage done by irrational dogmatism.

Unfortunately, in recent years similar damage is being done by highly sophisticated advocates of neo-orthodox theology in its more isolationist forms. Rebelling against the excessive accommodations of some liberal Christians to the characteristic tendencies of modern culture, but unwilling to join fundamentalists in their rigid Biblical literalism, some Christian teachers and ministers have sought to have their intellectual cake and eat it too. Discussing philosophy, the sciences, and history with the most learned representatives of modern culture, and accepting the most critical historical studies of the Bible, they have nevertheless insulated the intellectual content of their religious faith against all this learning. Teaching the radical discontinuity of revelation and everything human, they declare that Christian doctrine is not in need of any rational defense. It is simply to be declared and accepted " by faith." If this procedure results in inner contradictions, these inconsistencies are simply praised as the " paradoxes " inherent in the Christian gospel as seen by sinful men.

The evil results of such strategy are to be found on every hand. Declarations of faith and declarations of skepticism confront each other without even honest effort to find a common language of communication. At the very time when many universities are seeking eagerly for means of drawing together the diverse specializations of their departments into new cultural wholeness, religion becomes a new source of arbitrary and intransigent division. The hostilities that have resulted, on many campuses, between departments of religion or theological schools and the other departments to which Christian faith is being constantly set in " paradoxical " opposition, show that this is no mere theoretical peril. Whoever may profit from such an atmosphere of mutual suspicion and dogmatic isolationism, certainly truth and wholeness of life in individual and community are not advanced.

The need is not for a violent swinging of the theological pendulum from faith to reason. That could be more disastrous, even, than the present clamor for faith without reason. Neither the individual nor the community is to be saved by a faithless reason. The truth makes us free only when we move from thinking about it to devoted commitment to it. Not irrational faith or faithless reason is the need of the hour, but reasonable faith and faith-filled reason.

If such union of reason and faith is to be gained, it must not be as a mere device of propaganda. It must arise from a genuine conviction that the faith that is needful is the faith that is true. A man with such a conviction will make an end of all defensive religious isolationism. Any aspect of his present belief which is false he wants to discover and dismiss. He will have nothing to do with idols, however comforting or traditional. Only the God who truly is can be a fit object of his ultimate allegiance. Hence, every kind of data throwing light on the question of truth will be welcomed.

God's communication with which we are concerned is his communication to man. It is as human beings that we must receive this communication, recognize it, interpret it, and commit our lives to it. A man reading or hearing with understanding, distinguishing the true from the false, interpreting truth received and guiding action toward purposed ends, is a man reasoning.

Would we live by God's word of truth? Then we must dedicate our reason as the God-given instrument of its discriminating and understanding reception.

" Come now, let us reason together, says the Lord." (Isa. 1:18.)

II.

The Word and the Book

THE WORD OF GOD AND THE WORDS OF MEN

When the Christian thinks of God's word to men, his thoughts turn to the Bible. It is through the Bible that there has come to him the "good news" by which he lives. We must now consider the authority to be found in that book.

The authority of God is, of course, absolute. He is our Maker, the all-wise Creator, who holds in his power the destiny of us all. To obey his word is not to obey some mere external authority. He has made us for purposes best known to him. Our own self-fulfillment can come only in obedience to his word.

However, as already observed, communication always depends on the receiver as well as the giver of the communication. God's word spoken to us through the Bible depends for the clarity and purity of its reception both upon our own open and understanding minds and also upon the reception and expression given his word by the ancient men who wrote the words of the Bible and, in some instances, others who related orally the messages later written down in the Scriptures.

William Jennings Bryan, in his book *In His Image,* declared that the Bible was written either by men or by God. If written by men, there was no reason for us to believe any of it. If written by God, then every word of it was trustworthy. If Mr. Bryan had been better informed, he would not have made so rash a statement. Like many other fundamentalists he intended to defend the book sacred to him against the modern sciences which he mistakenly took to be its

46

deadly foes. Yet he and they, in taking such a stand, set up a line of defense impossible for any honest and well-informed person to defend.

We know that every last word of the Bible was written by men. Most of the Old Testament was written in Hebrew, with a small part in Aramaic, and the New Testament was written in Greek. The Bible was so written, not because God speaks these languages in preference to others, but because people who spoke Hebrew, Greek, or Aramaic wrote it. The very languages used bear witness to the times, places, and casts of thought of the writers, as surely as the language of the King James Version bears the mark of Elizabethan English. We even know the names of some Biblical writers, and concerning a few we have considerable personal information.

The Bible shows clearly that fallible men have written, edited, copied, and translated it. The history of Christian doctrine and the present schools of theological thought show also that fallible men have interpreted its meaning and must still do so.

The a priori argument of the Roman Catholic Church that God must have provided an infallible interpreter, the pope, with the infallible Bible, breaks down at three points. God does not always do as our abstract reasoning sometimes speculates that he must, and there is no evidence to indicate the actual provision of an infallible interpreter. Although the papal office has been filled by many consecrated and wise men, as well as by some scoundrels, their mutual contradictions, their violations of the most basic teachings of the Bible, and the presumptuous pride of their utterances show them to be far from infallible interpreters of Scripture. Besides, the Bible itself is by no means infallible. In it are to be found the erring words of men as well as the authoritative word of God.

The contrary accounts of chronology, numbers of soldiers, and other details show that the writers are prone to mistakes. Moreover, the religious significance of events can be the subject of radical disagreement by Biblical writers, as when one writer attributes the taking of a certain census to a command of God while another says it was by command of Satan. (II Sam. 24:1 and I Chron. 21:1.) In a few imprecatory psalms such merciless and bitter hate is expressed that John Wesley well said that these psalms were "highly improper for the mouths of a Christian congregation."[1] The cynical views of life and its senseless futility expressed by the principal writer of Ecclesiastes (e.g., Eccl., chs. 3 and 4) are so far beneath the level of both Jewish and Christian faith that later commentators apparently felt moved to insert pious protests and correctives (e.g., ch. 2:25-26 and ch. 12:13-14). Jesus himself challenged some commands of the Old Testament. (Matt. 5:21-48.) If it be argued that the old law as it stood was God's infallible word, but was later repealed and supplanted in the new dispensation, it must be pointed out that Jesus' words hardly accord with such a view. He gave reasons for his commands that had been as sound in the ancient days as in his own. (Matt. 5:33-37, 45.)

The plain fact is that the level of truth varies greatly in different parts of the Bible. Often the men of later times are prepared by earlier writings to receive new and higher revelations. Such an ascending scale is especially impressive in the stream of Old Testament prophecy, and as the New Testament employs the Old for its foundation. However, there is no such invariable progress that one should expect the later to be higher than the earlier. What Jew or Christian would prefer the relatively late Ecclesiastes to the much earlier writing of Isaiah, chs. 1 to 39? What branch of Christendom would choose the book of Revelation in preference to Paul's Letter to the Romans or the Gospel of Matthew?

The writings in the Bible are the writings of men, conditioned and limited by their times and their individual peculiarities, though also rising frequently to great heights of expression under the illumination of God's self-disclosing presence. The reader who would hear the true word of God in the reading of the Bible must be prepared to discriminate between the word of God and the words of men.

READING IN TOTAL CONTEXT

The untrained reader does well to read for the nurture of his spirit and not to become unduly concerned about passages that appear to contradict the spirit of Christ or the scientific knowledge of our times. There is enough to live by without specialized learning.

However, the theologian has the responsibility of searching out as much as he can and giving guidance to the church in its instrumental ministry. In varying degrees this more exacting task of serious study must be shared by ministers, teachers of related subjects in college or seminary, and teachers in local church schools. It is useful, also, to have increasing numbers of church laymen moving far into such studies for the enrichment of their own lives and for better leadership in the lay responsibilities of church and community.

For all who are to engage in this task of firsthand, serious, discriminating search for the true word of God through the words of the Bible, it is necessary that the words being read be seen in total context. This total context includes several dimensions of study and spiritual preparation:

1. *Literary Context.* First of all, every verse must be read as part of the larger passage in which it occurs. Sometimes, to be sure, the meaning will be clear in the one verse standing alone. However, often when it seems to be so, it will be found that the first impression was false and the meaning is radically changed by consideration of the whole passage.

One of the commonest errors in Bible study is the treating of single sentences, or even parts of sentences, as if they were all intended as theological propositions, to be used as building blocks in a system. Literalists employing this method suppose that any theological question can be settled by the quoting of single verses out of context. Often the users of this proof-texting method at the same time ignore or brush aside all contrary passages, while reiterating the texts that verbally support their positions and condemning all who differ with their interpretations as " doubting God's word."

Reading in context means not only taking account of the passage immediately surrounding the verse in hand; it means also considering this passage in relation to other passages in the same or different books that bear on the same problem directly or by implication. It is especially important that the student pay attention to passages that teach or at least appear to teach opposing doctrine. Some writers, like Paul, are so emphatic in style that if I read only one utterance on a subject, I may gain a highly distorted view of their teaching. When emphasizing one point he goes all out in stressing that as if nothing else mattered. At other times he often corrects the resulting imbalance by stressing opposite aspects of the truth. Only when one has read the whole of his writings on a subject has one a right to say with confidence what is Paul's teaching concerning it.

Recently it was my misfortune to be wedged in beside an argumentative stranger in a public limousine between railroad stations in Chicago. He saw that I had in my hand a theological book, and this was all the opening he needed. He asked whether I knew that if a man once professed his belief in Jesus Christ, he could never thereafter fall from God's grace. When I mildly demurred, he quoted John 3:16, and with an air of triumph he said, " So, you see, if you believe, you will be saved, no matter what happens after this." Gently I reminded him that the belief enjoined here was much more than a mere intellectual assent, for " even the demons believe — and shudder " (James 2:19); moreover, that we must beware of spiritual pride and presuming on God's mercy; that there are many Scriptural warnings against such proud presumption. " Therefore let any one who thinks that he stands take heed lest he fall." (I Cor. 10:12.) However, ignoring this and all other evidence from the Bible, he only quoted John 3:16 again, in plain disregard of its main intent, and repeatedly demanded to know if I proposed to " make God a liar " by " disbelieving His word."

If we seriously want to know the Biblical teaching on a subject, we need to sit down humbly before it and try to see together its varied approaches to the theme. We must read each passage in its own setting and in the light of the others. We must read in total literary context.

2. *Historical Context.* Much of the most careful and skilled scholarly labor has been devoted to establishing the true historical context of every part of the Bible. This work has included the minute, comparative analysis of the languages employed, archaeological research, hypothetical reconstructions of possible sequences of development in thought, and the establishing of every possible kind of relation with non-Biblical historical studies. Many problems remain unsolved. Yet it is now possible to fix the dates, places, and circumstances of many

Biblical books and passages within books, within limits much narrower and surer than could be done before the present century.

This historical study is carried on in close conjunction with textual criticism. Indeed, textual and historical criticism are so intimately linked as to be inseparable. Often the knowledge of the historical circumstances of a writing is decisive in determining which of various readings presented by ancient manuscripts is more likely to approximate closely the original. On the other hand, the determining of the correct text sometimes throws light on the historical circumstances of writing. The correcting of the text and the historical locating of the writing are but different aspects of one great task.

The intimate and inseparable relation between textual and historical studies of the Bible seems not to be adequately appreciated by some conservative scholars. For example, Edward J. Carnell praises unstintedly the devotion, skill, and results of textual criticism. He says:

> "What we possess in our present Bibles today is a remarkably substantial copy of this first set of writings, the purity of which is determined by the research of lower criticism. The lower critic must study the hundreds of extant Hebrew and Greek writings to determine which documents proceed from the original sources and which are spurious, for only the original writers, not the copyists and transcribers, were inspired. . . . Unless some objective science of criticism can be set up, Christians are left without a norm by which to tell God's genuine revelation from a corruption which has crept in." [2]

On the other hand, when the same writer considers the work of historical or " higher " criticism, he has nothing to say for it. Quoting from Edwin A. Burtt, he says of " higher criticism " that it

> " is the attempt to determine the meaning of the text, and to do so by the same methods that scientific investigation has found successful in dealing with secular writings." [3]

Then Carnell adds,

> " Observe that a fundamental presupposition of the higher critic is that the Bible is just another piece of human writing, a book to

which the scientific method may safely be applied, not realizing
that the Bible message stands pitted in judgment against that very
method itself." [4]

This is strange doctrine in a book that rests the whole case for a
conservative theology on the philosophical criterion of coherence.
He even asks,

"How can we tell the voice of God from the voice of the devil
if God does not maintain a relation to us wherein the laws of rationality are applicable to his revelation?" [5]

Here, then, is an author who believes thoroughly in the propriety
of applying "the laws of rationality" which are useful elsewhere
to the Scripture, who believes in applying the strictest scientific
methods to the criticism of the various textual readings, but who,
when he sees the effort to discover meanings in the text by relating
the words to the historical circumstances of their writing, protests
that this is to apply profane canons to sacred revelation!

Actually, of course, the textual criticism that is so highly praised
depends upon knowledge of the historical development of language
and the ideas conveyed by the language in various periods. Often
the decision between alternative readings depends in significant part
upon knowledge derived from the study of non-Biblical writings.
Textual and historical criticism are intricately interwoven with each
other and with non-Biblical archaeological, historical, and linguistic
studies. Even chemical and electronic knowledge may be usefully
brought to bear in determining the relative age of ancient manuscripts. So intimately connected are Biblical and "secular" science.

As we read any part of the Bible, in serious, scholarly effort to
determine its meaning with utmost precision, then, we must read in
the light of the historical situation out of which it issued and to
which it was addressed. The word given to us from on high was not
spoken to angels but to men. These men lived in specific places on
earth under particular historical conditions that determined the
language, cultural idiom, and patterns of ideas by means of which
they understood and conveyed the divine word to others. The better
we can recover an understanding of those historical circumstances

in which they heard his word and in which they or others wrote their interpretations of it, the more nearly we can approach the sacred Word itself.

Such men as Carnell and Cornelius Van Til have moved from the doctrine of verbal inerrancy of the Bible to the doctrine that although this present Bible has minor mistakes in it, the original manuscripts of the inspired authors were infallible. This is a step in the right direction. However, the original writers were also men, and so fallible. Another step is needed. God's own word alone is infallible. That is no more to be placed in our hands and read today than are the original " autographa " of which Van Til and Carnell write. But we can recover anew, today, the sense of that divinely spoken word. We more nearly approach that sacred word as spoken to men in ancient times as we are enabled to understand more precisely the quite human, historical conditioning of their response and testimony to it. The words of Scripture are to be read in historical perspective, that the word of God to their age and so, finally, his word to our age, may be more accurately and clearly understood.

3. *Christian Context.* Karl Barth makes a useful analysis of revelation when he speaks of " the Word as written," " the Word as preached," and " the Word as revealed." [6] God first addressed to ancient men " the Word as revealed." We now read of that Word in the Bible, or " the Word as written." However, the Bible does not fall to us from heaven; it is transmitted to us by the church through all its varied ministries which, together, Barth calls " the Word as preached." Moreover, we do not rightly understand the Bible if we seek to learn it in lonely isolation from the community of faith. " The Word as written " must be accompanied by " the Word as preached." However, I may read the Bible and hear the preaching with completely unmoved, insensitive heart, perceiving nothing but words and offense. If I am to understand rightly, " the Word as revealed " must be now renewed by God's living presence to me. He alone can make the words read and heard come alive to me.

One need not subscribe to Barth's doctrine as a whole in order to see the truth and importance of this analysis. The person who would understand well the life-transforming message of the Bible needs to be instructed concerning it in the community of faith, to share its treasures in the Christian fellowship, and to read in the mood of humble prayer for God's enlightening presence.

It is also exceedingly important that the Bible be read with the right questions in mind. Reading the Bible is not always a religious activity, just as songs about God and heaven are not always religious songs but may actually be blasphemous, and just as many sentimental pictures of Jesus are not religious art. Reading the Bible becomes a religious or even a Christian reading when we come to it with our deeper needs and concerns boldly and humbly bared to the word that God may speak to us through the words on the page.

Throughout our reading we need to be in quest for the illuminating, cleansing, transforming, life-giving Word that God speaks to us in Jesus Christ. Neither any Biblical writer nor the historic church has ever taught that we are saved by the words on the printed page. We are saved by the Word made flesh in Jesus. We read the Scripture in order that we may know him and that we may know him better. He gives to everything that came before and everything that comes after him its highest significance. To be sure, the Old Testament is a vast storehouse of treasures rightly cherished long before his coming. Yet its highest peaks of inspiration point toward Him who transfigures and fulfills all.

In short, we must read the Bible in the context of the Christian church, in the humility of prayer and of our deepest need, and in the hope of fulfillment in Christ.

4. *Total Perspective.* The Bible becomes most meaningful when read by persons well informed from other sources. Men of little faith sometimes fearfully seek to isolate the Bible from the main mass of human knowledge, as if in the hope that the word of God could thus be kept from contamination by the words of men. Such Biblical isolationism largely defeats the very purpose of revelation.

God's revelation is addressed to men in this world. If this communication is to succeed at all, the word of God must be received, interpreted, and obeyed by human beings. This is already evident in the nature of the Bible itself. This collection of writings is, as we have already observed, made up completely of human words spoken

and written in particular times and places of earthly history. Moreover, the revelatory events reported, the "mighty acts of God" by
which he disclosed his judgment and mercy to men, occurred in no
celestial spheres of action, but right here in the midst of earthly toil
and struggle. The Bible is full of marriages, births, and deaths, of
singing, grieving, traveling, fighting, buying, selling, eating, drink-
ing, and letter writing. We need not fear to bring the Bible into the
context of worldly existence. It was written here concerning events
and insights that God gave to men in the world.

To read the Bible with understanding today, the Christian needs
to be aware of many ancient conditions in the government, econ-
omy, social structure, and understanding of the world in Biblical
times. This is not because the culture and social conditions of those
times are superior in sanctity and should be transplanted into the
twentieth century. There is no need to establish a monarchy because
the Israelites lived for centuries under monarchies. We are under
no obligation to establish a Sanhedrin or to frequent bubbling pools
of water for healing in imitation of the first century. Many prescientific ideas about the world appear in the Bible as part of the
very language of the day. Only an ignoramus or a fool believes, in
the twentieth century, that the sky is a firmament — a solid dome —
over a flat earth, or that rain and flood result from the opening of
windows in the firmament and the unstopping of fountains from
under the earth. The describing of many diseases and especially
those of mind and nervous system as cases of demon-possession is
not sacrosanct just because it occurs frequently in Biblical accounts.
That was simply current medical thought and terminology among
many peoples as it is today among many tribes untrained in modern medical science. There is no more need for us to adopt such
ideas than there is to use only sailing ships on the high seas, as did
Paul, or to wear sandals, as did Jesus.

The more we know about the institutions and ideas current in
Biblical times, the better we can distinguish the kernel of divine
wisdom from the husk of transient human customs and ideas, and
the better we can understand the true meaning of the divine word
spoken among ancient men. In this process we need no diminishing

of modern scientific or historical learning. The more knowledge from every quarter we can bring to our reading, the better. Whatever we read that is contrary to our systematic, substantiated knowledge, we recognize as part of the dated human error. The illuminating meaning of the great events and the growing edge of insight given in the Scriptures stand well in the test of coherent understanding in this as in every age. Truth need not fear the most rigorous examination.

The testing of the Biblical materials by all we know of science and history has other values besides the aid in distinguishing the eternal word of truth from the dated error. By reading in the broadest context possible we also bring the leaven of God's word into the total mass of our thought and understanding. Only so do we open the complete man to divine illumination.

AUTHORITY IN SUCH CONTEXT

Many persons in our society use the Bible only for its apt putting of truths known independently from other sources. Such usage does not imply recognition of any Biblical authority.

At the other extreme are those who say they believe in the infallibility of all teachings in the Bible. Actually such persons show by their practice that they do not live by such a belief. For example, they accept the teachings of the New Testament that after death the faithful will be in heaven glorifying God (cf. Rev. 7:13-17), while they do not accept the plain teaching of Ecclesiastes that all men, good and evil, go to the same fate in death, for " the dead know nothing, and they have no more reward " (Eccl. 9:2-5). They make this choice wisely, but in doing so they are not believing in practice their theoretical doctrine that the Bible is infallible in every part. The doctrine of infallibility is quite impossible in practice, for one cannot put into living faith flatly contrary teachings.

There is high authority to be found in the Scripture, but this authority is not a general uniform authority of the words " from cover to cover." The authority of the word of God resides precisely in those teachings through which God speaks now to the living faith of the reader. God does not contradict in one disclosure of his truth what he affirms in another. The word of God spoken to us through the Bible does not contradict the word he has spoken through general revelation or the word that he now speaks in faithful hearts open to his presence. Yet, were it not for the events recorded in the Bible we should not have this living fellowship of faith through which God's love and our hope in him have been mediated to us.

We recognize, as we read the Bible, the very roots of the life which is to us life, indeed. Without the availability of the Bible here and now, we should be immeasurably impoverished. The reading of its pages renews our understanding of the faith by which we live as Christians. The teachings of the Bible, as tested in the life of the church, and in the open, critical thinking of innumerable devout scholars, call us back to the events through which the power of God came uniquely into human history for our salvation. By present study of the Scripture we correct our understanding of our faith and we renew our faith itself.

There is much in the Bible that is not essential to our salvation nor yet obviously dated and false. The association of such material with the word of God that we find in the Scripture predisposes the Christian in its favor. Yet the presence with it of much that is evidently human error keeps us from complete confidence in these borderline teachings. On such matters as the existence of superhuman personal creatures of God, for example, Christians can well afford to read reverently, think, and let think.

The authority of the Bible is not such as to be strengthened by isolation from all other authority. Throughout the history of Christendom, Christian scholars have organized total views of the world in which the sciences, philosophical inferences from the evidences of common human experience, and the teachings of the Bible have all been woven together in unity. Truth is one. When it is seen as one, it is both the more convincing and the more effective in the molding of life in all its aspects. The monumental systems of Augustine and Thomas Aquinas made possible an effectiveness of Christian faith in the Middle Ages that could not have been achieved otherwise.

At the same time there are dangers in this process. When Christian doctrine is commended to the world by a coherent apologetic system that includes many elements drawn from the culture of the times, it undoubtedly gains greatly in persuasiveness to that age. However, the science and philosophy of one age may become superstition and falsehood to a later period. At a time when men are disposing of discredited ideas, there is always a critical danger that they will also throw out other beliefs that have been intimately interwoven with them in thought and practice.

Another danger is that in the process of commending the Christian faith to the people of a particular culture, Christian teaching will be so largely accommodated to that culture as to lose its essential character and its saving power. For example, in proving the existence of God to his contemporaries by Aristotelian arguments, Thomas Aquinas came to represent God more as the timeless, unmoved perfection of Pure Form than as the living, freely acting Father who chose to reconcile us to himself through Christ. Similarly, in accommodating the gospel to the nineteenth and twentieth centuries, some Christians have so eagerly adopted evolutionary thought that they have displaced the Biblical challenge to crucial decision by an insipid gradualism. Then, when world wars and the awful threat of nuclear annihilation brought disillusionment, some theologians sought to wed the gospel to irrational despair and the complete separation of hope from God's moral commands and from history, as if there were neither law nor incarnation.

Some degree of accommodation to culture seems inevitable unless Christian teaching is to become a mere irrelevant echoing of ancient creeds — which were themselves products of some accommodation to Hellenic thought. This inevitability is clearly observable in American fundamentalism.

Fundamentalism was a revolt against liberal accommodation to modern culture. Its leaders were determined to return to the Bible, and they stood defiant to modern ways of thinking. Yet precisely because fundamentalism refused to enter into real two-way communication with the social sciences and because it failed to understand the moral significance of current social movements, it became the stanch ally of the most materialistic, nationalistic, and threatening foes of true Christian life in America. The lack of a prophetic social message has become of increasing concern to such conservative leaders as Harold Ockenga and Carl F. H. Henry, but their new magazine on social problems, *Christianity Today,* can still be counted on to defend a quite reactionary American isolationism in politics and the right of private exploitation of natural resources in economics.

The legitimate task of the Christian thinker is clearly to enter into genuine communication with the culture of his day, but to keep himself steeped in the historic teachings of the Bible and church. Such communication alone makes possible the realistic confronting of the men and women in a modern age with the claims and privileges of the gospel. As he carries out this task, the Christian must keep it constantly in mind that the one absolute authority is God himself, that he speaks to us through many channels, and that he speaks to us supremely in Christ, of whom we learn primarily through the Bible. Both our age and our own thought and life are answerable to God's judgment.

III.

The Word Made Flesh

SON OF MAN

According to the Synoptic Gospels, Jesus' favorite designation of himself was "the Son of man."[1] Sometimes the reference may be to the apocalyptic figure designated in Dan. 7:13 as "one like a son of man." However, the phrase is also used in the Old Testament to designate any man or man in general[2] and it is the common designation of Ezekiel in his prophetic visions.[3] Ezekiel probably conceived of himself in his prophetic role as representative man. The early church certainly thought of Jesus in this way, and he may have intended such a thought of himself at times when he called himself "the Son of man."

In this section, however, we are thinking simply of Jesus as a man, a son of the human race.

One of the earliest examples we have of Christian preaching is in the report of Peter's sermon on the Day of Pentecost. In that sermon Peter is reported as commending Jesus to his hearers as follows:

> "Men of Israel, hear these words: Jesus of Nazareth, a man attested to you by God with mighty works and wonders and signs which God did through him in your midst, as you yourselves know." (Acts 2:22.)

This is the Jesus of whom the church speaks, "a man attested . . . by God with mighty works," not just another man, but "a man," nevertheless.

To be sure, two of the Gospels say that he had no human father, but only a virgin mother. However, those are the same two Gospels, Matthew and Luke, which trace his ancestry through Joseph, transparently inserting phrases to bring verbal conformity with the doctrine of the virgin birth. (Matt. 1:16; Luke 3:23.) If he was miraculously born, it is apparent that the neighbors in Nazareth knew nothing about it. They spoke of Jesus as Joseph's son and found it hard to believe that this familiar home-town boy, now grown to mature manhood, could speak with such authority in the synagogue. (Matt. 13:54-56; Luke 4:16, 21-22. Cf. John 6:42.) Not only do Mark, John, and the epistles say nothing about the virgin birth, but John represents Philip as testifying to his Messiahship while calling him "Jesus of Nazareth, the son of Joseph" (John 1:45).

In any event, considering all the sermons and letters and the Gospels of Mark and John that we have in the New Testament without a mention of a virgin birth, it is evident that this doctrine was not essential to the church's message of salvation. Moreover, even if Jesus were born of one human parent rather than of two, this miraculous sign would not alter his essential humanity. Neither Gospel nor church has ever taught that God was the father of Jesus in the same literal sense in which Zechariah was the father of John the Baptist. In fact, the early fathers were at pains to condemn any such idea. Pagan stories of the gods seducing the women of earth were all too well known, and the Christians wanted it thoroughly understood that their Christ was not the child of any such union.[4] The term "Son of God" has meanings totally different from this.

Jesus was a man, born in weakness, growing in body, mind, and spiritual maturity, hungering, thirsting, sorrowing, rejoicing, suffering, praying "to him who was able to save him from death," and — though "he was heard for his godly fear" (Heb. 5:7) — dying "by the hands of lawless men" (Acts 2:23). He is not one "who is unable to sympathize with our weaknesses, but one who in every respect has been tempted as we are, yet without sinning" (Heb. 4:15). All three Synoptic Gospels tell of the temptations that he underwent at the beginning of his ministry.

It is no accident that so much stress is laid on Jesus' true and full humanity in the New Testament. It is to men and women, not to angels, that he mediated the revelation and love of God. Much of the wonder and usefulness of his revelation, in the eyes of the first Christians, derived from the fact that he was a man. He was not a demigod, nor an angel, but a human being sharing the temptations, grime, injustice, tears, and death to which we are subject. This is absolutely essential to our gospel.

SON OF GOD

There is a remarkable agreement of testimony in the New Testament that Jesus Christ is the Son of God. All four Gospels so designate him, as do The Acts, most of the Pauline Letters, the Letter to the Hebrews, and most of the remaining books. Every one of the authors whom we have cited directly or by implication as affirming his full humanity asserts also that Jesus is the Son of God — plainly in an altogether unique sense. Two truths, then, are suggested. First, the belief that Jesus is the Son of God is an essential element in the Christian faith as it is set forth in the New Testament. Of that there is abundant evidence. Secondly, the writers so conceive the meaning of this divine Sonship that they see no inconsistency between that and the most thoroughgoing humanity. In fact, the phrase " the Son of man " even suggests that he is man in his very essence, all the more man because he is the Son of God, perfect man in perfect Sonship to God.

This line of thought is worth pursuing further. In the account of creation we read that " God created man in his own image, in the image of God he created him; male and female he created them " (Gen. 1:27). A little later we read:

> " When God created man, he made him in the likeness of God. Male and female he created them, and he blessed them and named them Man when they were created. When Adam had lived a hundred and thirty years, he became the father of a son in his own likeness, after his image, and named him Seth." (Gen. 5:1-3.)

Notice that man was made in the likeness of God as Seth was made in the likeness of Adam. So Luke calls Adam " the son of God " (Luke 3:38). However, man as known in history is disfigured by sin, the likeness to God gravely scarred and deformed. As Jesus speaks to all kinds of people about God, he frequently speaks of him as "your Father," but while God has a Father's attitude to them they have not an attitude of filial loyalty or obedience toward him. They are not his children, in their eyes, though he is their Father, in his.

Jesus, on the other hand, is God's faithful son. Living in conscious reliance upon God, he subjects his own will to the Father's will. In him history makes a new beginning. The divine likeness is clearly seen in him. He is " the second Adam " (cf. I Cor. 15:22, 45) Among the men known in history Jesus alone is truly the Son of God.

Jesus, in his controlling center of motivation and purpose, not only stands closer to God than does any other man; he is capable of being fully understood only by God, and God can be properly known only by those who are enabled to do so by Jesus. " All things," Jesus says,

> "have been delivered to me by my Father; and no one knows the Son except the Father, and no one knows the Father except the Son and any one to whom the Son chooses to reveal him." (Matt. 11:27; cf. Luke 10:22.)

That Jesus is the Son of God in this unique sense is manifested in many ways, according to the New Testament account. In all three Synoptic Gospels a special point of emphasis is made of his authority to forgive sins. (Mark 2:7-12; Matt. 9:2-7; Luke 5:18-25.) Many are the reports of his miraculous healings. John tells of his raising Lazarus from the dead. Matthew, Mark, and John tell of his walking on the Sea of Galilee to meet the storm-tossed boat carrying his disciples. (Matt. 14:22-33; Mark 6:47-51; John 6:16-21.) The three Synoptic Gospels tell of his rebuking a storm on the same body of water, so quieting the wind and waves. (Mark 4:35-41; Matt. 8:23-27; Luke 8:22-25.) The feeding of the five thousand and the changing of the water into wine at Cana are likewise doubtless intended to show his divine authority over the forces of nature.

Further regarded as God's own testimony to Jesus' unique Sonship are the miraculously announced virgin birth, the Voice from heaven at his baptism, the transfiguration and the Voice from heaven on that occasion, the darkening sky and earthquake at his crucifixion, and above all, his resurrection from the dead and finally his ascension into heaven.

The New Testament, while in these many ways emphasizing Jesus' unique relation to God, with his consequent authority and power, is remarkably reticent concerning the precise nature of this relationship. On occasion Jesus is represented as solemnly speaking of himself as "a prophet" (see Luke 13:33), and many times, especially in John, his subordination to God is emphasized. The development of his life from infancy to mature strength has already been mentioned. (Cf. Luke 2:40, 52.) On the other hand, he is described as existent before all things and as participating in their creation. (E.g., cf. Col. 1:15-19; Heb. 1:2; I Cor. 8:6; John 8:58.)

Little light is thrown on the relation of these various ideas. About as highly developed a statement concerning the ontological status of Christ as we have in the New Testament occurs in Phil. 2:5-11. Here three stages appear in sequence, the first stage being that "he [Christ Jesus] was in the form of God," but he "did not count equality with God a thing to be grasped," as he entered the second stage — the incarnation. He "emptied himself, taking the form of a servant, being born in the likeness of men." Even that did not mark the end of this humiliation, for "being found in human form he humbled himself and became obedient unto death, even death on a cross." However, the acceptance of this humiliation, in obedience to God, led to his third and final stage:

> "Therefore God has highly exalted him and bestowed on him the name which is above every name, that at the name of Jesus every knee should bow, in heaven and on earth and under the earth, and every tongue confess that Jesus Christ is Lord, to the glory of God the Father."

This, however, does not go far to satisfy a curious and speculative mind. Of what prerogative and powers did the Son empty himself in becoming man? What is the link of identity between the heavenly Son and the humble human servant? Are they really the same person? Is there a linkage of memory? Is the identity in self-consciousness at all? What is the relation, precisely, between the heavenly Son and the Father? All such questions remained to puzzle and stimulate many minds in the church for centuries. To some of them we must return in this study.

In the last century, however, the church has been shaken deeply by questions of a different order, having to do, not with the heavenly figure of the pre-existent or the glorified Son, but with the historical man, Jesus of Nazareth.

THE HISTORICAL JESUS

In the nineteenth century many New Testament scholars applied newly mastered techniques of historical cricitism to the Gospels in high hope of recovering for modern times a clear and adequate understanding of the true character, works, and teachings of Jesus. As the work continued into the twentieth century, increasingly grave misgivings developed concerning the possibility of bringing such an enterprise to a successful conclusion. The solving of this particular problem by methods of objective historical research is fraught with extraordinary difficulties. Paul Tillich even goes so far as to say that it is not only impossible to recover a historically defensible life of Jesus, but that even a delineation of his basic character or personality is altogether beyond our reach.[5] Of course Tillich favors historical research for other purposes, but he holds that "the attempt to give a foundation to Christian faith and theology through historical research is a failure."[6]

Such extreme pessimism concerning historical research is unwarranted. It is true that a consistent and detailed life of Jesus is impossible to construct from the materials we have. Of course, Tillich is also on solid ground when he insists that even as regards "a minimum of reliable facts about the man Jesus of Nazareth," historical research can achieve only historical probability, not to be identified with certainty, nor yet with the certitude of faith. But this does not imply that historical research applied to the New Testament cannot "give a foundation to Christian faith and theology."

It implies only that historical research *alone* does not provide a *sufficient* foundation for Christian faith and theology. The Christian faith — hence theology also — is rightly founded on the New Testament, understood with the aid of historical research, but also on the existence and history of the church, on the already demonstrated power of the faith to answer human need, and on a decision of will, not without evidence but in view of the probabilities evidentially established.[7]

Only by some such relationship between historical research and our faith can the nature of Christianity as a historical religion be continued. Albert Schweitzer wrote, in *The Quest of the Historical Jesus,*

" The Jesus of Nazareth who came forward publicly as the Messiah, who preached the ethics of the Kingdom of God, who founded the Kingdom of Heaven upon earth, and died to give his work its final consecration, never had any existence." [8]

Yet Schweitzer could minimize the importance of this supposed discovery, for he thought that it affected " only the brick facing of the real immovable historical foundation which is independent of any historical confirmation or justification." [9] However, " the solid foundation of Christianity," Schweitzer insists, the " fact " that " can neither be shaken nor confirmed by any historical discovery," is this: " Jesus means something to our world because a mighty spiritual force streams forth from him and flows through our time also." [10]

Is this not itself a historical fact? Is not this living power of the Christian ecclesia itself traceable back through history to the life of Jesus himself? Is this not precisely what Schweitzer affirms as immovable fact? How, then, can we know that this " mighty spiritual force streams forth from *him* " — that is, Jesus — without knowing that Jesus lived in history and that he was such a person as historically to give rise to just this movement?

The difficulty arises largely from the fact that very nearly all the historically useful narrative or interpretation concerning Jesus that we have available is the material in the New Testament, and all this material represents points of view acceptable to the church that preserved it. It was not written as objective history but as testimony and exhortation. Moreover, some assumptions of New Testament writers regarding natural causation and miracles, proper exegesis of the Old Testament, demonological explanations of illness (as compared with bacteriological and other accounts of medical science), cosmology and the imminent intervention of God to end the age, are not shared by many present readers. To reconstruct the ancient events and teachings in such a way as to make them meaningfully acceptable to us, we must somehow " demythologize " the accounts, to use Bultmann's useful term. However, there is then the problem of determining what is only mythical form, and what is part of the unique reality of the Christ-event.

While the resultant problems are difficult and will doubtless leave much in doubt and controversy, this does not mean that nothing can be learned from historical research that will positively support our faith as well as help to form our theological thought.

" The certitude of faith does not imply certainty about questions of historical research "[11] any more than faith implies certainty concerning any other intellectual problem. Historical research can, nevertheless, distinguish the historically probable from the historically improbable and so give guidance to our reasonable faith.

One fact that historical research must never forget, if it is to perform its proper function, is that the Christian movement, with all its creative power, did erupt into history from the historical Jesus. In weighing the probabilities of various alternative portraits of Jesus relative to the evidence, we must always include consideration of the probability that such a movement came from a life of this or that kind. To portray Jesus as an ordinary man without intellectual, moral, or spiritual distinction and then explain the rise of faith in him simply as a paradoxical work of God is to write history as badly as to explain other historical events by a *deus ex machina*, rather than with some concern for the continuity of historical events.[12]

The Jesus of history is a Jew of Nazareth, son of Joseph the carpenter and his wife Mary, well instructed in the Hebrew Scriptures and deeply concerned with his people's hope of deliverance from their sore trials and sin by the action of God. In his mature young manhood he heard the preaching of the prophet John the Baptist, who preached that the hour of deliverance and of God's reign was imminent, and called on all who would enter the divine Kingdom to repent of their sins, be baptized, and live in obedience to God's commands. Jesus became a prophet also, and he too announced that God's reign was at hand. He spoke of God's condemnation of sin, but stressed his fatherly care. He called on all who heard him to accept God's love, in humble trust, and to serve him by rigorously honest, pure lives of obedient love, confronting others, even others who despised and abused them, with generous, forgiving, helpful love. He identified himself and the message he preached as the culmination and fulfillment of the old age of the law and the inauguration of the new age of inner loyalty and love in which God's reign would be real. This divine reign would finally become fully manifest.[13]

His assuming authority to correct and complete the law, his identification of himself with the inauguration of God's reign, and his sharp denunciation of exploitation in the Temple at Jerusalem brought upon him the wrath of the priests and the conservative Pharisees of his nation, while the rigor and enthusiasm of his religious teachings repelled the worldly-wise Sadducees. At the same time, his broad human sympathies, his generous ministry to the most despised people, and his healing of many sick persons attracted crowds and won the affection of the classes most despised and feared by Pharisees and Sadducees alike. From just such crowds might at any time come disorders that would for no good purpose bring down upon Jerusalem the crushing retribution of Rome.

The forces hostile to him, by a combination of appeal to the mob and stirring the anxiety of the local Roman rulers, soon succeeded in having him arrested and, after some difficulties, securing his conviction and crucifixion. Shortly after his interment, he was repeatedly reported as having been seen and having participated in intimate fellowship with various individuals and groups of his associates.

Many of his specific sayings are recorded in the Synoptic Gospels and, after the most rigorous critical studies, stand well authenticated as in all probability substantially his own. They show his thought to have been in the great Hebrew prophetic tradition. More or less similar sayings parallel to each of his ethical teachings can be found elsewhere in Hebrew literature. However, the *Gestalt* of his teachings is radically new, in its combination of stress on unlimited, forgiving, sacrificial love, inward purity of heart as contrasted with legal observance, and the relating of his teaching to his own role in inaugurating the new age of God's reign. This last aspect became more prominent still among his disciples. So completely did they identify the whole meaning of the righteous life as he portrayed it with his own personal career that the main subject of their preaching became his personal life, crucifixion, and resurrection.

The Christian church is not a school of thought nor yet a cultus. It is not primarily a body of men held together by believing in certain ethical ideals or religious ideas taught by Jesus — though these teachings have had and now have a very important place. The rites of the various branches of the church and the world views held by them differ in the extreme, even among those bodies which find priceless Christian fellowship in the modern ecumenical movement. All regard themselves first of all as being held together by faith *in Christ*. They constitute a continuance in history of the new divine creative power and love that came into the world in Jesus. They are " the body of Christ."

Jesus Christ is, then, both a historically datable life — the Jesus known to history — and also the living reality without such limitation in time. In the Jesus of history God commanded and some men obeyed. But that is not all. As Albert Schweitzer, even at the end of his *Quest*, with all its negative results — unduly negative as they now appear — testifies in the closing sentences:

> " He speaks to us the same word: ' Follow thou me! ' and sets us to the tasks which he has to fulfill for our time. He commands. And to those who obey him, whether they be wise or simple, he will reveal himself in the toils, the conflicts, the sufferings which they shall pass through in his fellowship, and, as an ineffable mystery, they shall learn in their own experience who he is." [14]

In many ways the church, through the centuries, has testified to this eternal Christ, the Christ known to faith in every age since Jesus' coming. All its works of love have been part of that testimony. It has also testified in sacrament and music, in ritual and art. Here we must be concerned especially with the testimony in theological statement. What, then, has the church said of the eternal Christ?

THE ETERNAL CHRIST

In the Apostles' Creed, as it stood in the fourth century, apparently after long use, there is nothing explicit about a pre-existent Christ, the second article beginning, " And [I believe] in Jesus Christ, his only Son, our Lord; who was born by the Holy Ghost of the Virgin Mary." [15] However, the place of Christ after the earthly life of the historical Jesus is clearly affirmed, in the words,

> " The third day he rose from the dead; he ascended into heaven; and sitteth on the right hand of the Father; from thence he shall come to judge the quick and the dead." [16]

This is in accord with the place of Christ in human experience. There was no human knowledge of such a one until Jesus' historical life, though his disciples then regarded him as having come from God in a unique sense, as the Apostles' Creed suggests. However, after the earthly ministry of Jesus, his followers found, and still find, in their religious experience, a high place for the ever-living Christ; indeed, in Christian thought and experience Christ has a place very closely related to that of God himself. Christ says to us, as to the Evangelist of the late first century, " He who has seen me has seen the Father " (John 14:9). The Christian cannot think of God without including in the conception his knowledge of the teachings, work, and person of Jesus. Jesus, as thus associated in our thought and religious experience with the Father, is appropriately described symbolically as sitting " on the right hand of the Father." Moreover, since he is the norm of all human life, it is appropriately said that from this exalted place of authority with the Father, " he shall come to judge the quick and the dead."

As within the New Testament the place of the historical human

Jesus in the faith of the disciples led to the attribution of ever more divine prerogatives and divine properties to him, so in the continuing thought of the church such development persisted. Thus, in the Nicene Creed, as enlarged in 381, at Constantinople, we read:

> " And [we believe] in one Lord Jesus Christ, the only-begotten Son of God, begotten of the Father before all worlds; Light of Light, very God of very God, begotten not made, being of one substance with the Father; by whom all things were made; who, for us men, and for our salvation, came down from heaven, and was incarnate by the Holy Ghost of the Virgin Mary, and was made man." [17]

Again, after the affirmation that he " sitteth on the right hand of the Father," there occur further elaborations in the statements,

> " And he shall come again, with glory, to judge the quick and the dead; whose kingdom shall have no end. And in the Holy Ghost, the Lord and Giver of life; who proceedeth from the Father; who with the Father and the Son together is worshiped and glorified." [18]

Here the contrast with the New Testament is marked. While the New Testament declares that Christ is one with the Father and glorifies him in many other exalted terms, it stops short of an absolute and unequivocal identification of Christ with God himself. Even the Gospel of John, which affirms the unity of Christ and the Father, represents Christ as praying for the same unity among his disciples. (John 17:11, 21-22, 26.) The Nicene-Constantinopolitan Creed, on the other hand, casts aside all restraint in declaring that Jesus Christ is " very God of very God . . . of one substance with the Father." Thus the experiential unity of love, purpose, and understanding represented in John, ch. 17, becomes, in the thought of the fourth century, an outright metaphysical identity, even while, paradoxically, a distinction is still made.

The Council of Chalcedon, in 451, had yet to deal with the relation between the eternal Son and the historical man Jesus. It did so by declaring that Jesus was " perfect in Godhead " and " perfect in Manhood; truly God and truly Man."[19] The Two Natures, human and divine, were said to be distinguished, with their "differences . . . being in no way removed by the Union," yet both "inseparably" united "into One Prosopon (Person) and One Hypostasis."[20]

This paradox was affirmed, in the philosophical language of the day, because the revelation received by Christian faith seemed to require it if a metaphysical declaration were to be made at all. Speculation in such terms was going on inevitably, and the line between the heretical and the proper declarations of faith had to be drawn in terms relevant to both. Jesus was known beyond doubt to have been a historical human person. Yet in him God had done great things for man. To the action of God in Christ the church and its people owed the very life and faith to which they were bearing witness. It was not some angel or demigod, much less a mere man who had been revealed in the man Jesus, but the one true God, Creator of all things. In the very interest of monotheism and of their living faith they declared the unity of God with man in Jesus. Though we be unable to share their Hellenic ontological categories or to regard their statement of paradox as a satisfactory interpretation of the person of Christ for our age, we may yet share their concern and the faith that they expressed in terms that seem now so ponderous and needlessly self-contradictory.

Further comments must be made on appropriate and inappropriate distinctions between the Jesus of history and the Christ of faith. Literally to worship the man Jesus of Nazareth would be idolatry. Yet in the traditional liturgy of the church and in present religious experience of Christians — even when so unorthodox as an Albert Schweitzer — "Christ" is One who "speaks to us the same word: 'Follow thou me!' and sets us to the tasks which he has to fulfill for our time."[21] "Christ" here appears in present experience as God. This Christ as God is not to be *confused* with Jesus the man of Nazareth. At the same time this Christ is *inseparable* from the man Jesus. It is the historical Jesus who has supplied us, by his very person, with all our most adequate understanding of God himself.[22] Hence there come inevitably to our minds the words of the Chalcedonian formula that acknowledge Jesus Christ "in Two Natures unconfusedly, . . . inseparably."[23] As an ontological theory the Chalcedonian Creed, with its ancient metaphysical categories, is quite impossible for most of us. Yet as an expression of our apprehension of God through the man Jesus it speaks for our faith, as for theirs in the fifth century.

There is more in the mysteries of faith than can be comprehended adequately in any of our concepts. Yet we, too, must attempt to declare our Christological faith in concepts meaningful to our own times. For this purpose we may well take our clue from the Prologue to the Gospel of John.

THE WORD MADE FLESH

When the Gospel of John represents Jesus as the human embodiment of "the Word," a term of rich historical connotation is being employed. That Jewish philosophical contemporary of Jesus, Philo of Alexandria, employed the term Word, or *Logos,* in a way that was significant and influential. In his usage it meant the structured thought of God conceived as issuing forth from him to become a mediating reality through which God created the world and through which he is related to the world. The *Logos,* for Philo, then, fulfills the metaphysical function of Plato's eternal Ideas, conceived as united in one structure; and at the same time it serves as a mediator between the transcendent, mysterious, perfect God and the imperfect yet largely intelligible world.[24]

The word is also prominent in the Old Testament. It was by God's spoken word that all things were created. (Gen., ch. 1.) It was also his word that came to the prophets. (Cf., e.g., Jer. 1:2, 11, 13; 2:1, 4.) When the word of God came, it brought not only the substance of the prophet's message, but also the compulsion, courage, and power to deliver it. So Amos writes, "The Lord God has spoken; who can but prophesy?" (Amos 3:8.)

Jesus too was a prophet. (Cf. Luke 13:33.) He too was "preaching the word" (Mark 2:2). But he was more than a prophet. He not only spoke the word. He was the same word. His words revealed much of God's goodness, love, and glory. His life revealed even more. In the human Jesus "the Word became flesh and dwelt among us, full of grace and truth" (John 1:14).

God was revealed to Jesus, it is true, and the New Testament represents, without equivocation, his dependence upon God for guidance, for power, and even for his salvation. (Cf. John 5:30-32; Heb. 5:7.) At the same time, the vocation to which he was called and his freely chosen faithfulness to it were such that he came to be thought of principally as the revealer. So clearly did he stand between other men and God and so truly did his very person indicate the likeness and direction of God, that in looking to him men found and men still find themselves looking to God. So completely did he freely give his speech, his deeds, and above all his very being into God's use, that God spoke through him and acted through him. His speech was God speaking; his loving deeds were God's own acts; where he was, God was dynamically present in power.

Jesus was no mere puppet. He was every inch a man, the more completely man because he was wholly yielded by his own free will to God. He both fulfilled man's rightful destiny, by being thus yielded to God, and also showed to other men God in action in the life of man. In him the will of a man and the will of God met and became one in purpose for the redemption of sinful, lost humanity.

THE CROSS

An emphatic part of the Christian gospel from the beginning has been the teaching that "God shows his love for us in that while we were yet sinners Christ died for us" (Rom. 5:8).

In the New Testament it is not explained why or how the crucifixion of Christ accomplished the release of men from guilt and sin. Indeed, in the Gospels this release is described as the mission of his life and his teaching as well as of his death. Thus, when the Pharisees complained of his association "with tax collectors and sinners," Jesus replied, "Those who are well have no need of a physician, but those who are sick; I came not to call the righteous, but sinners" (Mark 2:17). He said in Nazareth that in him was the fulfillment of Isaiah's prophecy:

" The Spirit of the Lord is upon me,
because he has anointed me to preach good news to the poor.
He has sent me to proclaim release to the captives
and recovering of sight to the blind,
to set at liberty those who are oppressed,
to proclaim the acceptable year of the Lord." (Luke 4:18-19.)

In the home of Zacchaeus he declared: " Today salvation has come
to this house. . . . For the Son of man came to seek and to save the
lost " (Luke 19:9-10).

Theologians have often stressed the death of Christ to the virtual
exclusion of interest in his life and teachings. It is easy to accept
Jesus' death as a substitute for righteousness in our own lives. If
" Jesus paid it all," then we go free without responsibility. But Jesus
warned, " Not every one who says to me, 'Lord, Lord,' shall enter
the kingdom of heaven, but he who does the will of my Father who
is in heaven." (Matt. 7:21; cf. Luke 6:46-49 and James 1:22.) Paul
laid great emphasis on the death of Christ, and he is quoted most by
those who would minimize Jesus' life and teaching. Yet he gives
much ethical instruction that echoes the teaching of Jesus, and he
writes pointedly to the church at Corinth,

" Do not be deceived; neither the immoral, nor idolaters, nor
adulterers, nor homosexuals, nor thieves, nor the greedy, nor
drunkards, nor revilers, nor robbers will inherit the kingdom of
God." (I Cor. 6:9-10.)

If one takes seriously the *whole* testimony of the New Testament,
two teachings about the cross of Christ frequently neglected in the
churches and in theology will be made emphatically clear. One is
that the crucifixion of Jesus is significant as climax of his *life* and
teachings, not in isolation from them. The other is that faith in the
cross of Christ can release men for righteous living; it does not release them from the responsibility for righteous living. (Cf. Matt.
16:21-26; I Cor. 6:11-20; Rom. 6:5-13.) People who are looking for
salvation at bargain prices can find many appealing advertisements
of it in current theology, but they will find small comfort if they
read the New Testament as a whole. Faith in the New Testament

sense includes loyal, obedient commitment to the life and teachings of Jesus as well as acceptance of his death in our behalf.

The fact remains that to his death is attributed very great importance. Why? The Gospels tell of Jesus' foretelling his death (see, e.g., Mark 9:31; Luke 9:22), and John represents him as saying, " I, when I am lifted up from the earth, will draw all men to myself " (John 12:32). How his crucifixion will " draw " men to him is not said, though it certainly has drawn many, after first driving some away. Paul describes the cross as God's wisdom and power (I Cor. 1:23-25), but he is testifying to the experienced fact as one who had tried to conquer the Christian movement and had been conquered by the crucified Christ, without attempting to explain. Paul speaks also of the death of Christ as fulfilling his righteousness by which men are made righteous. (Rom. 5:15-19.) Sometimes Paul thinks of Christians as participating in Christ's death or " in a death like his," in order to be raised also to new life with him. Baptism is regarded as symbolizing this death and resurrection of the believer. (Rom. 6:3-11. Cf. II Cor. 5:14-15; Gal. 2:19-20.) Again one sees here Paul's testimony to his own traumatic experience on the Damascus road. There he had yielded to Christ, thus " dying " to all that had been his life's purpose. There the struggle of self-assertive, self-dependent righteousness, with its proud condemnation of all that appeared false or evil in his eyes, ended in unconditional surrender. Having thus died to the old self, he was now raised in new and victorious life, symbol and promise of the resurrection yet to be when death had been left behind and eternal victory had been won. Yet never does Paul tell why Christ's death was necessary or helpful for this purpose.

The Fourth Gospel, by calling Jesus " the Lamb of God " (John 1:29, 36), suggests that Jesus is a sacrifice for sin. This theme is developed as the main teaching of The Letter to the Hebrews. There Jesus is represented both as the high priest who makes the offering for us and also as the sacrificial offering itself. If it is not apparent to us how such a bloody sacrifice would accomplish our redemption, it does seem to the ancient author, trained as he had been in the tradition of the sacrificial cultus that " without the shedding of blood there is no forgiveness of sins " (Heb. 9:22; cf. ch. 9, *passim*).

Like Paul, we must base our own theology of the cross upon the fact that lives have actually been profoundly changed and sanctified by confronting the cross and there surrendering themselves to Christ. The number of such persons has grown through the centuries to become, in truth, " a great multitude which no man could number, from every nation, from all tribes and peoples and tongues " (Rev. 7:9). We can stop there, like most of the New Testament writers, expressing wonder and gratitude for this great sanctifying power which God has released in the world through this most unlikely event, the crucifixion of Jesus. Sooner or later, indeed, we shall be compelled to stop silent before this mystery, for no explanation given is fully satisfactory. Yet we must say enough, at least, to disclaim some theories often given and sometimes supposed to be essential to Christian faith.

Certainly we ought to repudiate the notion that God is unwilling to forgive any sin until blood has been spilled as propitiation. There is powerful symbolism in ancient and modern sacrificial rites, but the service they have rendered has been required by men and not by God. The whole New Testament declares that God loved human sinners before Christ died. Indeed, Christ's mission is everywhere attributed to God's prior love. He was not waiting to be reconciled to men. Men needed the change of heart, not God. We may well concede, in the presence of the cross, that Jesus suffered what we, not he, deserved, and that because he suffered thus we have been changed and are being perfected in his likeness. Because he so identified himself with sinful men and suffered the foul blows of human hostility, we are saved from the worse death of sinful bondage and despair. In that sense he is a substitute for us. However, this is not a legal transaction required by God, in which God demanded his pound of flesh and took it from Christ instead of from us. Neither the New Testament nor experience supports such a view, and it would contradict violently the whole conception of God taught in the New Testament.

No more should we accept the theory, so popular in the early centuries, that Jesus' death was a payment by God of a ransom to

Satan for the release of men from bondage. It is true that the New Testament speaks of Jesus' life " as a ransom for many " (Matt. 20:28; Mark 10:45) or " for all " (I Tim. 2:6). But there is here no suggestion of a bargain between God and Satan, no mention at all being made of Satan. There is only the idea of Jesus' forfeiting his life for the sake of men. The notion of God's bargaining with Satan is inconsistent with the belief in the divine sovereignty as well as a gratuitous affront to reason. It implies an *ultimate* dualism of power in the universe which would deny the very basis of such ultimate trust in God as the New Testament teaches.

On the other hand, the idea that the power of the cross represents simply the lure of a courageous loyalty to high ideals is grossly inadequate. Certainly the cross has that power. The life and death of Jesus constitute a high revelation of what man may be, by the help of God. We find many appeals based on Jesus' courageous and sacrificial example in the literature of the first centuries. Indeed, such appeals are present in the Gospels themselves. (E.g., see Matt. 20:26-28; Mark 10:42-45; Luke 22:24-27.) But the predominant appeal and power of the cross has to do more directly with the relation between man and God.

Since it is man and not God who obstructs the right relation between man and God, let us ask, then, what power the cross has exercised to change men and reconcile them to God. Several factors in this power will be mentioned here. Doubtless there are others.

First of all, the crucifixion of Christ discloses the despicable blackness of men's sin, just such sin as we find in ourselves. At the cross we see with stark clarity that our sin is not a private nor only a human concern; it is enmity to God. Such insight is the first requirement of such repentance as can remove the barrier of guilt that stands between us and God. Yet this awareness of our own sinful rebellion is not enough. This alone might drive us into bitter despair. Such despair would be making explicit our actual desperate plight and so far would be good.[25] But if it is to lead to repentance, one thing more is needed.

At the cross of Christ we are assured of God's forgiving love. That assurance gives us hope that we may secure forgiveness and release from our guilt and sin.

A distinguished psychologist of my acquaintance, who has suffered extraordinarily over many years, tells me that to him the most wonderful thing about the crucifixion of Jesus is not God's forgiveness. It is the fact that " Jesus forgave God." Even in the terrible injustice and agony of his last hours Jesus did not curse the injustice of God.

Of course neither Jesus nor any New Testament writer would entertain for a moment the idea of forgiving God. But Jesus did accept his suffering and death as the righteous will of God, and this is profoundly significant. At the very least, Jesus knew God more intimately than do we. If he who knew him so well could take all the torture of crucifixion and yet so trust as he did the sovereign God who did not rescue him but willed that he should drink this cup, then we can trust him also. Jesus, in his dying agony, cried out, " Father, into thy hands I commit my spirit! " (Luke 23:46).

Then we, however deeply lost in guilt and bound by sin, can entrust to God our complete confession and surrender.

Moreover, if Jesus saw his own suffering as the way by which God's love was being given to sinful men, surely we too should understand it so. To understand the cross in this way is to give up any bitter resentments we hold because of real or fancied wrongs that we ourselves have suffered. Often such resentments have a large part in keeping us proud and stiff, "head . . . bloody but unbowed," in the presence of the loving Father who alone can relieve our aching hearts and put purpose into our empty meaninglessness.

This conveying of God's faithful love to us, together with the disclosure of our sin in its abysmal depths, brings the sinner to repentance, hence, forgiveness and new life, reconciled to God.

Did the death of Christ, then, accomplish nothing new, but only reveal God's love as it had been all along and man's sin as it always is? William J. Wolf, in his useful study entitled *No Cross, No Crown,* strongly repudiates such an idea. He writes:

> " It is not a question here of mere revelation. The cross in deepening guilt at the same time actually conveys love to the sinner and enables him to respond with a love made the more spontaneous and less self-regarding by being the grateful love of a guilt forgiven." [26]

The phrase "mere revelation" here is unfortunate, though I think the meaning is clear. The cross is not a mere teaching of a truth about God. God acted in Christ, so that it was his own purpose and action that men condemned when they crucified Jesus. God shared profoundly the suffering of Jesus for the sake of the sinners who put him to death and all other sinners too. No revelation of God is a mere making known of a new idea. All revelation of God is a self-disclosure in which he gives himself in some way to the recipient.

The crucifixion of Jesus powerfully conveyed the love of God to some men and women who received this gift in faith. Through the continued working of the Holy Spirit this love formed a new community of love and forgiveness, and that in turn has continued to convey this forgiving love to others down through the centuries and out through the world. The cross has changed the historical situation for us all who have been touched by this living stream.

For no man is the work of the cross automatic. To us as to the people gathered on Calvary it is a crisis, a new occasion of profoundly significant decision. In criticizing the theories of moral influence, Wolf actually says truly concerning the cross of Christ, however interpreted in theological theory:

> "Unless God leads me into the redemptive fellowship in the context of which I can see that his Son's death speaks to my situation and to the situation of my fellow men, I cannot see the point. The assumption that a display of costly love will always create gratitude is simply not true to the harsh facts of life." [27]

The crucifixion of Christ is not just a "display of costly love." It is also tragically true that the cross of Christ, even when made known, does not "always create gratitude." It did not do so in all on Calvary, and it does not do so in all who are told of it today. The community of faithful men is bound not only to reach out in every discoverable way to men of imaginations sensitive to the depth of Christ's suffering for them, but also to convey Christ's love to the dull and prosaic in ways most meaningful to them. But it still remains true that for many the cross is only foolishness or a stumbling block, while for some who, enabled by God's grace, freely respond in faith, it is the saving love and supreme wisdom of God.

In the earliest literature of the church, the crucifixion is usually presented in close relation to the resurrection. Sometimes, indeed, the death of Jesus seems little more than preparation for his resurrection. The importance of this connection must not be neglected.

It must be granted that the disconnected, contradictory, and strange evidence we have does not make it possible for us to construct a clear, intelligible account of precisely what happened on the first Easter morning. It is clear, however, that the disciples — and Paul — encountered the living Jesus as a triumphant, commanding person, in such a way that they could not doubt his living presence. This experience assured them that because he lived they too would live if only they shared his mission and his death. It also showed unmistakably that he represented the authority of God in all his life, and that his death, so far from being his defeat, was part of God's mighty act in him.

As we can see especially clearly in Paul's writing on the cross, the very mystery of this revelation had an important part in his salvation. That God would use the crucifixion of the Messiah for his own good purpose was impossible to explain according to any of Paul's familiar legal or eschatological categories. The shattering effect of his encounter with the living Christ was the greater because it was so completely baffling. He could not fit this into his old life and thought at all. He could accept it only by unconditional surrender. Such surrender was exactly what was needed if God was to forgive and refashion him as his apostle to the Gentiles.

To us, also, the cross is mystery that shows us how little we are able to comprehend our needs and God's ways. Yet we have not only the ancient testimony to the resurrection, but also the centuries of church history and the millions of restored and transformed lives to show that God was, in truth, acting in our behalf on Calvary and at the open tomb. When we bow in complete surrender before this mysterious revelation of God, we receive God's forgiving and transforming grace. Then when we return to reconstruct our understanding of God, the world, and ourselves, we find such coherence of meaning as could not be found before. Then, like Paul, we know and preach

> " Christ crucified, a stumbling-block to Jews and folly to Gentiles, but to those who are called, both Jews and Greeks, Christ the power of God and the wisdom of God " (I Cor. 1:23-24).

We have not to do, here, with ultimate contradiction or incoherence. We have to do, rather, with a revolution of both being and thought profounder than the Einsteinian revolution in natural science, but like it leading to a rich coherence much greater than could be reached by the use of old hypotheses and categories.

PART TWO
GOD'S PRESENT CONCERN FOR US

IV.

The God Who Speaks

MYSTERIOUS

The God who reveals himself to us is One who is and must remain for us veiled in mystery. We are accustomed to thinking and talking of things and persons capable of identification in terms of spatiotemporal perception. God, on the other hand, is unseen. Of his presence, as of his Kingdom, we are unable to say, "'Lo, here . . . !' or 'There!'" (Luke 17:21). He is always out of sight and beyond comprehension.

The Athenians erected an altar "To an unknown God" (Acts 17:23). He is not so to Christians or to men of the Old Covenant. Yet throughout the Bible his hiddenness is often emphasized. Although Moses can see his glory when he has passed by, God tells him, "You cannot see my face; for man shall not see me and live" (Ex. 33:20). Not only to sense perception is he hidden, but also to understanding, especially in our darkest hours of suffering and grief. Job speaks for the many when he complains:

"Behold, I go forward, but he is not there;
   and backward, but I cannot perceive him;
on the left hand I seek him, but I cannot behold him;
   I turn to the right hand, but I cannot see him." (Job 23:8-9.)

Truly, "clouds and thick darkness are round about him" (Ps. 97:2), even in the hours when we are gratefully conscious of his reign.

In the midst of eternity, we have lived but a few years since birth, and even the history of all mankind is only a moment in astronomical time. How should we understand the darkness from which we came and into which we soon go at death? The mystery is too great for us. Out of the mystery God has spoken to us, and so by his will we know him. Yet even as we know him the mystery remains. Some *men* are largely beyond my comprehension. The composer-conductor of a great symphony, carrying in his mind, indeed constructing there, all that complex score and all the intricate tonal tapestry woven by one hundred instruments, is quite beyond my ability to imagine. One such musical genius has tried to tell me about the experience of composing. Yet, though such self-disclosure tells me much, the composer remains to me mostly a mystery. How infinitely more the Creator of the universe — composers and all! — must remain always heavily veiled in unfathomable distance for our limited minds.

This inherent, overwhelming hiddenness of God must not be forgotten as we stand in wonder before his self-disclosure. Only as we remember the depth and darkness of the mystery shall we with sufficient awe and gratitude receive the revelation. Only thus shall we be possessed by that fear of the Lord which is the beginning of wisdom. However well known, the one God, when truly encountered, is confronted as the *mysterium* and *tremendum*,[1] never as one comprehensible, clearly definable, and comfortably familiar.

Yet Known

The wonderful truth is that the God who surpasses our understanding has revealed himself to us, even to our understanding, in many ways. The "unknown God" is the self-revealed God who can be proclaimed with confidence to all men. (Cf. Acts 17:23.)

He has disclosed himself "in the things that have been made" (Rom. 1:20); in the norms of truth, beauty, and goodness engraved in the human heart, however disfigured; in the mighty acts of revelation to which the Bible testifies; and in those encounters with us in the depths of our own hearts which we call religious experience. He "did not leave himself without witness" (Acts 14:17) among any people. There is no nature nor human nature without grace.

The stamp of the Creator and Sustainer is upon all things and all men, however much else may obscure it.

The meaningful relations of stars, crystals, and subatomic structures correspond remarkably to those systematic developments of man's own mind which we call pure mathematics. It is a fact of great significance that the man who has done most to unlock the secrets of the physical world to human understanding and control, in this century, is Albert Einstein, who was engaged principally in abstract thinking about pure theory. When man's mind thinks most vigorously and clearly, being faithful only to the norms of its own nature, it is able to penetrate most deeply into the character of the external world. The beings and events that are needed to complete the schemes of a theoretical physics are found, again and again, actually to exist. Just so, in 1846, the planet Neptune, which no one had observed but which was needed to complete man's formulas, came into the field of the telescope right on time, as if the universe were obliged to fulfill the requirements of man's rational schemes. There is evidently an inner kinship or likeness between the human intellect at its best and the controlling power of the physical world. Through the visible things of nature God thus reveals one important aspect of his own being.

It is important that too much not be claimed for such evidences. When Thomas Aquinas " proves " the " existence of God " by proving that there is a First Mover or a First Cause or a Necessary Being, he assumes too much.[2] If we accept, for example, his proof of the First Cause, that First Cause might be some kind of being otherwise altogether unknown to us and having no other attribute of *God,* so far as Thomas' second proof is concerned, excepting only the being First Cause. Similarly, when we have seen that the structure of natural processes implies a controlling reason, this does not prove that such reason has all the other attributes of *God,* as the Christian thinks of God.

Nevertheless, it is exceedingly important that there is evidence strongly favoring belief in a reason actively controlling the natural processes, a reason analogous to human reason at its best. We may call such cosmic reason " X," if we like, rather than " God." But we are then free to inquire what other attributes " X " must have.

If the cosmic " X " is a reason actively controlling the structures of natural process, we must regard that " X " as being able to project its own meanings in action. This is precisely what we mean by a rational will. " X," then, is to be regarded as a being characterized by reason and will.

Moreover, " X " has somehow given rise to the strange and interesting being we call man. How should it happen that among the rocks, plants, and animals of this planet there should be this thinking, restless mammal who is not content with securing his mere survival, but counts certain abstractions, such as truth, goodness, liberty, and justice as so priceless in value that they are worthy of many an expenditure of life itself? This restless seeking after ideals is deeply joined with man's ability to understand the rational structures that confront him in his natural environment. If he had no love of truth and beauty, and no capacity for conscientious, disciplined honesty, patience, and co-operation, there would be no science. To understand the world's structures man needs not only his best reason, but also his best honesty, his self-disciplined love of truth, and his capacity for patient co-operation. Such *moral* ideals as these, along with his intellectual best, are required to correlate his thought with the secrets of the cosmic " X." It is seen, then, that as man's own searching reason probes for the secrets of the world, " X " is meeting him with the highest demands upon his moral as well as his intellectual best. The revelation-discovery of science takes place only when man meets the requirements of the " X " which he is moving out to meet. These requirements are both intellectual and moral. This fact favors the belief that of all things of which we know the one that is most akin to " X " is man at his rational and moral best.

From this point on we should be entitled to call " X " *God.* For the guiding, rational will controlling the world process and *en rapport* with man at his rational and moral best would be universally known as *God,* even though much that the Christian believes about God is not revealed in these considerations about nature and our scientific knowledge of it.

PERSONAL

God has also disclosed his own nature in all that cumulative body of revelation to which men have borne witness in the Bible. Here, too, he is revealed as reason and will, a personal Being most like man at his best, but much more specific meaning is given to the divine character and purpose for man. He is the God of righteous judgment and love. Indeed, his judgments, which sometimes appear to men in the guise of wrathful severity, are expressions of his love. (See Hos., *passim;* also Heb. 12:5-11.)

It is strange that in recent Christian theology there is doubt expressed, not uncommonly, about the propriety of describing God as personal. Of course for many centuries various philosophers have thought the world-ground to be impersonal and sometimes they have spoken of an impersonal universal substance or world-ground as " God." However, the Christian Scriptures, liturgies, and practice of prayer so plainly imply that God is personal that it is incongruous to find among Christian theologians reluctance to affirm that he is personal.

Sometimes the objection is that to call God personal is to imply that he is subject to human limitations. It would be altogether irrational to regard him as so limited. God is from everlasting, while we are, both individually and collectively, of recent origin. God has created all the galaxies measured in light-years, while we can hardly find expression for our pride that we have at last been able to project into space some objects measured in inches, by the use of energy and materials that God has provided. God gives the laws by which nature abides, while men must learn these laws by observation and interpretation. God is the very source of righteousness, while men fall far short even of that limited righteousness which they envision and to which they fitfully aspire. The God who knows and cares for each one of his children on this planet, while sustaining also all the vast universe, is infinitely beyond our imaginations, let alone the limits of our own being.

When it is declared that God is personal, it is affirmed that, *whatever other attributes he may have,* he is *at least* able to know and to will. Granted that we cannot imagine what it would be like to be aware of all events everywhere, to sustain the whole world-process, and to have power to act without limitations of space, it is apparent that such awareness and will are like powers of our own spirits heightened to the nth power and completely free from limitations imposed by any such bodies as ours.[3] If God were not a purposive, willing being who knows what is going on, he would be less than we, and not the God who creates and acts upon his creation according to his loving purpose. The modes of his perception, reason, love, and will are doubtless unimaginably more than ours. But they *are* more and not less than ours. With all his vast powers, known and unknown to us, he is *at least* personal. In the same sense we may speak of him as the divine Person, not for a moment implying that he is *limited* to the attributes of a personal being such as we know in the human spirit. When some writers deny that God is personal, on the ground that to be personal is to be limited as God is not, the effect is to declare him impersonal, which is to say subpersonal. A force that is blind, purposeless, unknowing, is plainly of no value to itself. There can be meaning and value only to mind. To believe that man is the only being capable of thought and appreciation is to make all meaning and value anthropocentric. Theocentrism requires the belief that God is personal, though without limitation to the attributes of human persons.

In many ways the Bible teaches that God is personal. He created, and as he created he perceived what he was creating and appraised it as good (Gen., ch. 1). Peculiarly characteristic of conscious personal being is the declaration, " I am." Indeed, the Latin first person singular pronoun is often used to signify specifically the personal subject, as when we speak of the " ego." According to Ex. 3:14, God declared himself the unconditional Person, unqualified by dependence or by admixture with alien influences such as we find in ourselves. " God said to Moses, ' I am who I am.' "

One of the chief attributes of God as known to the great prophet of the exile whom we know as the Second Isaiah is his forward-looking purpose — the primary mark of personality. God revealed to the prophet:

> ". . . I am God, and there is no other;
>   I am God, and there is none like me,
> declaring the end from the beginning
>   and from ancient times things not yet done,
> saying, ' My counsel shall stand,
>   and I will accomplish all my purpose.' " (Isa. 46:9-10.)

The New Testament is especially rich in its teachings of the personal God. Jesus' favorite mode of reference to him declares him to be his Father and our Father. Even though God is perfectly righteous while all men are sinners, Jesus draws out the analogy between God and human fathers.[4] The God portrayed in the New Testament perceives his children at prayer and responds to them; he remembers, commands, declares his will, judges, warns, punishes, forgives, and loves. All these activities are plainly personal.

In one especially interesting passage, Paul explicitly describes God as a conscious, introspecting Person analogous to a man observing and reporting his own thoughts:

> " For what person knows a man's thoughts except the spirit of the man which is in him? So also no one comprehends the thoughts of God except the Spirit of God." (I Cor. 2:11-12.)

It is clear that the God portrayed in the Scriptures and revealed in Christ is a Person, whatever other attributes he may have, unknown to us.

Every moment of prayer by anyone in any age, in faith that God understands and responds, is a reaffirmation that God is personal. Even the simplest Christian believer understands this.[5]

Loving Father

To the Christian, God is known not only as personal but also as the particular loving Father who acts in history on our behalf, and especially as the love incarnate in Jesus Christ. God is no abstract universal, whether the Platonic Good or a generalized spirit of love. He is the particular loving Person who, as Creator, is the ground of all being and source of all meaning. Hence the validity and relevance of all abstract universals that truly represent reality are rooted in him. He is the Particular ontologically prior to all universals.

Jesus speaks truly to the experiential faith of the believer in the words, " He who has seen me has seen the Father " (John 14:9). The words, deeds, and life of Jesus in history are the Word of God disclosing himself in his particular character, purpose, and power. In Jesus the character of God is seen as love. His purpose is to love and so to redeem his children. His power is the power of love.

To declare that " God is love " is to affirm a mysterious and wonderful faith. There is much in the world that seems to contradict it. The sufferings of children dying of cancer, the wasted life of idiots, the devastations wrought by earthquakes, hurricanes, and floods, do not look like the work of a loving God. Youth who in adolescence become estranged from themselves and lash out in desperation against those who love them, men and women whose lust seeks to use each other's bodies with wanton disregard for the dignity of selfhood, races and classes of people who deny their common humanity in divisive injustice and fear, and nations of men who devastate the earth and threaten total mutual annihilation in war — these do not look like the children of a loving Father.

These are not all we see. There are also devoted nurses caring tenderly for the sick and incompetent. There are medical scientists searching arduously, patiently, and co-operatively for cures and preventives of disease. Every natural disaster is an occasion for heroic exploits of courage, generosity, and labor unrequited excepting by the fulfillment of love's demands. The youth who drive their parents nearly to despair by their self-defeating rebellions also pierce through superficial conventions to ask ultimate questions and rise to glorious heights of inspiration and responsible self-sacrifice. Men and women present sexual desire as a sacramental offering by which human life is ennobled in holy wedlock and heavenly love is foreshadowed. The fear, injustice, and hatred of classes, races, and nations call forth from many persons such heroic and prophetic devotion to truth, righteousness, and peace as to sanctify even the abyss of desolation that others have made.

There is much in our world that no man has found a way adequately to explain. Yet rival hypotheses are not equal in adequacy.

This is not a world in which good and evil, love and hate, enjoy equal status. Love and purity bring harmony and peace. They are at home in the very character of the universe. Hate and lust are self-destroying. Whether within the individual or in the community, they bring strife, discontent, and disaster. They must defy the sanctions of the very ontal structure of the world. Much of the worst pain and waste of human life is the fruitage of human sin — though often not the sin of the persons who suffer most. We are bound strongly together, and our good or evil wills profoundly affect the whole community in which we participate.

An attractive idea, in relation to all such evidence, is a dualism of good and evil cosmic forces. Such a dualism is affirmed by Zoroastrianism and seems to have influenced somewhat the New Testament, especially some passages in the Gospel of John (e.g., see John 1:4-9), although perhaps little more than in the terminology of light and darkness. The terrible evils of the twentieth century and the disclosures of depth psychology have revived among serious thinkers an interest in demonology as explanation of evil. In the writings of most contemporary theologians who speak of "the demonic" and of superhuman "principalities and powers," it is difficult or impossible to determine how much is only figurative expression for the evil side of human motivation, individually or en masse, or for the experienced fact of evil in the world, regardless of explanation. Few responsible thinkers care to espouse an effort literally to account for particular instances of disease or natural disaster by reference to invisible, evil, superhuman personal beings at work in the world. When such explanation is attempted, as by Karl Heim,[6] the result hardly commends itself to critical thought.

To be sure, we cannot prove that there are not other evil minds and wills besides those of evil men, and it is conceivable that such evil creatures could have power to affect us, much as powerful evil men can so devastatingly affect other people. But the explanation of sickness and other "natural" evils by demonology has not only been, in the development of human thought, a theoretical dead end; it has led to many of the most wretched episodes of superstition and cruelty in human history. The witchcraft delusions, mixing of foul potions, baptizing of bells, and abuse of the mentally ill, which have been produced by demonology in the past, suggest that we would do well to be critical of such ideas today. We would best regard the belief in demons reflected in the New Testament as belonging merely to the pseudoscience of the first century, part of the erroneous human culture to which and through which the revelation came, and not as part of the revelation itself. In a general account of the evil in the world, the *possibility* of disrupting influences from erring wills other than human cannot be ruled out and may occupy a minor explanatory role. The history of scientific and religious theory and practice indicates that such ideas are both unfruitful and vicious when given prominent attention, dogmatic affirmation, and specific application.

In any event, an *ultimate* dualism of good and evil is contradicted by the overwhelming evidence that the universe is one system, ruled by one mind, not by two or more conflicting minds. Any dualism that falls short of being ultimate falls short of explanation. If evil is due to the evil work of demons or of a Satan created by God and ultimately under God's control, however rebellious against him now, then the question why God permits such evil creatures to harass and betray us remains. In short, an ultimate dualism is contrary to the evidence, while a dualism not ultimate is only a stopgap explanation.

Although there is much in our experience that remains mystery, even when our best thought has been long devoted to it, it does not follow that we should declare our faith irrational or nonrational. Despite the evils that remain unexplained, the view that God is good, that his goodness is love, and that his is the supreme power, is, on the whole, the most adequate of the explanatory doctrines that men have conceived.

All the evidence that God is love is immeasurably heightened in Jesus and his church. In Jesus the most wretched errors, religious fanaticism, cruelty, and hate met the most sublime love. Although Jesus faced all this evil in terrible human solitude and went to death before his enemies who were armed with the power of the mighty Roman Empire, yet the power of his love outmatched all. This power which he declared and his disciples believed to be the power of God in him, was vindicated when he was raised from the dead. The vindication continues in the life of the faithful Christian community. His disciples continue to testify that when they are weak, yet in him they are strong, for he has overcome the world.

ORDERLY GOVERNOR

The sciences, the common experience of mankind and the ancient writers of the Scriptures, alike acknowledge that the universe in which we have been placed is, on the whole, an orderly system. The inorganic processes, from the movements of the stars to changes within the atom, lend themselves remarkably to mechanistic description. Living things require further principles of description, so that biology cannot be fully reduced to physics and chemistry. Yet the biological realm, too, has its orderly regularities of reproduction, growth, and death. Neither biological mutations nor electronic indeterminacies obscure the overarching and dominant regularity of the world.

In all this vast order God makes himself known to us as the dependable and faithful Governor of the world, which he has created. We ourselves are of this world, as well as in it, and with all the rest of God's creation we are subject to his orderly government.

Spiritually, as well as physically, we are subject to this orderly rule. Our subjection is made evident in two different ways: First, there are causal laws in the realm of our mental processes as well as in the physical order. Psychology and psychiatry confront greater difficulties and narrower limitations than biology and medicine, but their achievements and further possibilities are admissible only because they, too, are working in a realm of causal order. Secondly, our wills are subject to obligations that are not, like causal law, coercive, but that are morally inescapable. We are not *compelled* to be honest, loyal to our ideals, or generous toward our neighbors, but we *ought* to be.

Amid the vast social movements of our times, much is changing and uncertain. Yet God still declares to us, as to the Hebrews of old, " I the Lord do not change " (Mal. 3:6). On the surface everything is insecure. In the depths there is solid ground on which we can stand firm by faith. Even our understanding of God's command-ments changes. Yet we can declare with the ancient poet,

> " The sum of thy word is truth;
>   and every one of thy righteous ordinances endures for ever "
> (Ps. 119:160).

FREE PROVIDENCE

Many conservative Christians recognize as God's own acts only those events which appear to violate or to transcend the regular or-der of nature. To such persons God is the miracle-worker who breaks into this world on special occasions rather than the constant, orderly Governor.

It is well that most thoughtful Christians have come to know, with Tennyson, that though " He thunder by law the thunder is yet His voice." [7]

Now, however, much religious thought has moved to an opposite distortion of the truth. Accepting gladly the doctrine that God is orderly Governor, whose action we see continually in the regular causal order of nature, many people have ceased to believe that God can act and does act at particular times, in particular places, in be-half of particular people. God has been so thoroughly identified with law that in much thought he has become nearly indistinguish-able from it.

The Bible contains many references to particular occasions on which God revealed his presence and spoke to individual people. Isaiah could report, " In the year that King Uzziah died I saw the Lord " (Isa. 6:1). Can we believe that such a vision as Isaiah had on that occasion was veritably due to a particular act of God's will? Can particular events in our own lives be regarded as the work of God, freely acting now as in ancient times?

Undoubtedly there are sound objections that ought to be pressed against our presuming to identify our own interpretations of par-ticular events with the purposes of God. Jesus warned against such a procedure in two specific instances:

"There were some present at that very time who told him of the Galileans whose blood Pilate had mingled with their sacrifices. And he answered them, 'Do you think that these Galileans were worse sinners than all the other Galileans, because they suffered thus? I tell you, No; but unless you repent you will all likewise perish. Or those eighteen upon whom the tower in Siloam fell and killed them, do you think that they were worse offenders than all the others who dwelt in Jerusalem? I tell you, No; but unless you repent you will all likewise perish.'" (Luke 13:1-5.)

A minister who, when a neighboring church was struck by lightning and considerably damaged, preached a rousing sermon on the judgments of God against worldly churches, put himself in a highly vulnerable position. When his own church was struck, a short time later, and burned to the ground, his embarrassment was well deserved. We need to show some humility before the mysteries of God and certainly to avoid attributing all our own prejudices and hostilities to him.

On the other hand, when a Saul of Tarsus reports a vision on the Damascus road and there follows a transformed, creative life that changes the course of history and brings multitudes to living faith, we may well join with him in attributing the vision to a purposeful act of God. In our own times, too, there are testimonies to divine visitations. When the events are followed by such changes of character and other consequences as are fittingly to be expected from divine action, we may well consider the testimonies with sympathetic favor.

The God in whom we believe as Christians is no mere system of law nor yet a helpless prisoner of the structure he has created. He is a Person who chooses to maintain an orderly system but who is also free to act within that system. It would be ironical, indeed, if, in a world where his humble creatures are free to express their wills within limits broad enough so that they can make quite perceptible differences on the face of the earth, the Creator were incapable of any such free expression of his purpose. The idea that he is powerful in the creating and sustaining of the world system, but powerless to act now upon any particular life, comes from loss of full faith in the personal God and Father revealed in Christ. The God who in particular times and places spoke by the prophets and supremely revealed his eternal Word in Jesus ministers also today in particular ways both to and through men and women of faith.

TRANSCENDENCE AND IMMANENCE

In Christian history theological thought has swung back and forth between emphasis on the transcendence of God and on the immanence of God. Some writers have represented God as so utterly different from man and so completely separated from this world of trouble and sin as to be altogether veiled in mystery. Others have stressed his never-failing faithful activity within the world and his presence to the human spirit.

Both emphases are indigenous to the Christian faith. When we accept the testimony of Scripture and experience in full perspective, we acknowledge that God is both transcendent and immanent.

In his holiness God so far surpasses us that he is altogether beyond the bounds of our sense perception, imagination, or adequate conception. The ancient Hebrews represented in many ways the awful gulf of difference that separated them from God. They taught that no man could see God and live. Where his presence was concentrated, as at the Ark of the Covenant or in the Holy of Holies, no approach could be safely made excepting by certain designated persons and by them only after solemn preparation and on rare occasions. Even the self-revealing God remained also the hidden God of mystery.

> " He made darkness his covering around him,
> his canopy thick clouds dark with water." (Ps. 18:11.)

The great prophet of the exile was not the only one to complain to him, " Truly, thou art a God who hidest thyself " (Isa. 45:15).

God is the majestic sovereign of all being. He is " the high and lofty One who inhabits eternity, whose name is Holy " (Isa. 57:15). His creative work, his wisdom, his righteousness, his ageless being from before all worlds, his invisible presence — all are signs of his transcendence.

Most recent theological writing has acknowledged all this readily enough. It is the immanence of God, his presence in the world and in human affairs, that seems now to be the stumbling block. Reacting violently against an earlier tendency simply to identify God with the laws of nature and the processes of history, some recent theologians have gone to the far extreme of denying that God is present in the world at all excepting in Jesus Christ and to Christian faith. The very word " immanence " is now, in some theological discussions, a term of opprobrium. The immanence of God is regarded as a false and alien notion imported into Christian theology from Greek philosophy or from modern idealistic metaphysics.

Actually, the transcendence of God is often stressed in the Biblical testimony precisely in order that there may be better expressed the wonder of his presence and availability. For example, the last passage quoted above, from Isa. 57:15, reads in full as follows:

> " For thus says the high and lofty One
>   who inhabits eternity, whose name is Holy:
> ' I dwell in the high and holy place,
>   and also with him who is of a contrite and humble spirit,
> to revive the spirit of the humble,
>   and to revive the heart of the contrite.' "

The church has always affirmed the omnipresent activity of God, and this belief is imbedded deep in the Bible. This doctrine clearly implies the immanence of God. Webster's Dictionary defines immanence in the theological sense as meaning " the indwelling presence of God in the world (including man)." Sometimes the term is so used as to imply that the regular processes of nature are his own activity. Note, then, how completely the divine immanence is affirmed in the following words:

> " If I ascend to heaven, thou art there!
>   If I make my bed in Sheol, thou art there!
> If I take the wings of the morning
>   and dwell in the uttermost parts of the sea,
> even there thy hand shall lead me,
>   and thy right hand shall hold me. . . .

> For thou didst form my inward parts,
>   thou didst knit me together in my mother's womb."
>   (Ps. 139:8-10, 13.)

Similarly, Jesus speaks of the Father's making " his sun rise on the evil and on the good," and the rain fall " on the just and on the unjust " (Matt. 5:45). Likewise, he ascribes the beauty of wild flowers to God's present activity. (Matt. 6:28-30.)

Paul was teaching the ancient doctrine of his Hebrew ancestors and was faithful to the instruction of Jesus when, in Athens, he said of God, " He himself gives to all men life and breath and everything " (Acts 17:25). Hence he did not balk at quoting the Stoic poet Epimenides' affirmation of the divine immanence: " In him we live and move and have our being " (Acts 17:28).

When the writer of the Fourth Gospel describes the wonder of the incarnation, he does not speak of it as of God's light and power entering into a world to which he was alien or from which he had been long withdrawn. Rather, he says:

> " The true light *that enlightens every man* was coming into the world. He was in the world, and the world was made through him, yet the world knew him not. He came to *his own home,* and *his own people* received him not." (John 1:9-11. Emphasis mine.)

Cyril C. Richardson contends that the doctrine of the Trinity is an attempt, never altogether successful, to express the paradoxical nature of God. Of the various antinomies involved in our thought of God, says Richardson, " the most basic one concerns that of contrasting God in his absolute character, or mode of being, from that of God as he is related to his world." [8] Some antinomies can be resolved, but not this one.

> " Here we meet an antinomy, an essential paradox. There is no way of overcoming it, and we must leave it at that. . . . That is the way God is — absolutely transcendent, single, simple, unveiled, inaccessible, and infinitely above his creation; yet, too, he is related to it. He creates, he manifests his love and enters into the realm of suffering for our redemption. . . . Everywhere we confront the paradox; nowhere can we resolve it. There is no

third term by which to compose it. Yet it is basic to our faith. We can sacrifice neither God's absolute transcendence, nor his intimate relation with the world. To abandon the one is to say he is not really God; to abandon the other is to say he is not the God of our world." [9]

As an interpretation of the doctrine of the Trinity in its basic intention and significance, Richardson's view may be questioned. I shall have more to say about the Trinity later. Just now I am concerned with the necessity to true religion of affirming both the transcendence of God and his "intimate relation with the world," that is, his immanence.

In the Scriptural testimony, there is undoubtedly a certain tension between the idea of transcendence and the idea of immanence. However, in the Bible the distinction is not made such an irresoluble and irrational paradox as Richardson points out in some later Christian thought.

The transcendent God disclosed in the Bible is not represented as unconcerned or unrelated. To be sure, he is represented as not requiring to be "served by human hands, as though he needed anything," but the next clause shows that he is not regarded as unrelated: "since he himself gives to all men life and breath and everything" (Acts 17:25). The relations between God and man are never denied, but are irreversible. He does not depend upon men for his own being; we do depend upon him for ours. Motivated by abstract theoretical concerns, Christians have often denied that God needed human beings even for the full expression of his love. But this is not affirmed in the Bible.[10] It is doubtless implied that he can make creatures at will, and hence his love has always its own power of expression, both in the power to create and in the further ability to love his creatures. As for the God that is "beyond suffering,"[11] or the thought of God in terms of the "Greek Absolute" or of his "final transcendence over against his relatedness," Richardson himself acknowledges that such attempted understanding of the Father "could never be satisfactory to a theology oriented toward the Scriptures."[12] In the Scriptures "the intimate relation of the Father with his world was too clear to make such a delimitation of the first two terms [Father and Son] cogent." [13] Exactly. But this does not show that the doctrine of the Trinity was poorly adapted to serve its purpose. Not only is the primary purpose of the doctrine *not* to resolve the antinomy of the impassable, unrelated God and the deeply involved, suffering God who is ever near; the impassable, unrelated God does not exist for the main Scriptural witnesses.

Indeed, a striking fact of Biblical teaching is that the doctrine of divine immanence is there made ontologically dependent upon the doctrine of divine transcendence. Hence, affirmations of God's immanence in the world testify to his transcendence. The very teaching that "he himself gives to all men life and breath and everything" is proof that he "does not live in shrines made by man, nor is he served by human hands, as though he needed anything" (Acts 17:24-25). The psalmist tells of God's immanent activity as he says,

" For thou didst form my inward parts,
    thou didst knit me together in my mother's womb " (Ps. 139:13).

But this acknowledgment leads him immediately to declare,

"I praise thee, for thou art fearful and wonderful" (Ps. 139:14).

Paul reminds us of Aristotle's efficient cause, formal cause, and final cause, as he unequivocally declares the immanence of God in his creation: "For from him and through him and to him are all things" (Rom. 11:36). But the verses leading up to this declaration speak in awe of his transcendence:

" O the depth of the riches and wisdom and knowledge of God!
How unsearchable are his judgments and how inscrutable his ways!
    ' For who has known the mind of the Lord,
    or who has been his counselor? '
    ' Or who has given a gift to him
    that he might be repaid? ' " (Vs. 33-35.)

Then, right after the affirmation of the divine immanence, Paul praises him in terms properly addressed to a transcendent deity: " To him be glory forever. Amen " (v. 36).

When Deutero-Isaiah exhorts the wicked,

> " Seek the Lord, while he may be found,
>   call upon him while he is near " (Isa. 55:6),

he is soon supporting this affirmation of God's immanence and available mercy by stressing his transcendence:

> "For as the heavens are higher than the earth,
>   so are my ways higher than your ways
>   and my thoughts than your thoughts." (V. 9.)

It is precisely because God is infinitely secure and strong that he is able to love so purely and involve himself so humbly with us in our sin and suffering. Only the God whose ways of knowing and caring unimaginably transcend our own could know each one of his earthly children in tender concern. Only the omnipotent God who is mysterious to our weakness could be omnipresent. Only he who transcends all bounds could be he of whom it can be said, that " he is not far from each one of us, for

' In him we live and move and have our being ' " (Acts 17:27 28)

The transcendence of God passes all our understanding. Yet it does not pass our understanding that only a God of just such transcendent greatness, so far removed from our own limitations, could be always so near, so aware of our innermost thoughts, and so sensitive of our every need as faith affirms God to be in his immanence.

V.

The Triune God

Testimony to Historical Revelation

The doctrine of the Trinity is a testimony to God's communication with man. Only in this perspective may it be properly approached and understood.

Although the Trinitarian creeds have been formulated in the categories of speculative metaphysics, the basic motivation of Trinitarian thought is religious and historical. The Christian faith is a profoundly historical religion, rooted not in abstract speculation but in testimony to self-revealing acts of God. It is fitting, therefore, that the Christian doctrine of the Trinity should be a symbolically condensed history of revelation. As R. S. Franks writes, the doctrine of the Trinity

> " sprang from the reaction upon Jewish monotheism of belief in the divine mission of Jesus Christ and the experience of the power of the Holy Spirit in the Christian church. Since Jewish monotheism itself is traced by Christians to divine revelation, there are three fundamental acts of God in history, the recognition of which forms the basis of the doctrine of the Trinity." [1]

Many of our young ministers view the doctrine of the Trinity as an unfortunate embarrassment. They think of it in terms of ancient creeds couched in the technical language of Greek metaphysics. It seems foreign, self-contradictory, remote from experience, alien to Biblical testimony, and contrary to all sound reason. Some of them even think it a denial of monotheism, or at least a threat to it. Remembering that Jesus emphatically reaffirmed the Hebrew Shema, they conclude that they ought to be Unitarians. For they too believe that " The Lord our God is one Lord."

How ironical all this would seem to Tertullian, Athanasius, and Augustine! The very doctrine that was fashioned to *affirm* the unity of God is now widely regarded as a threat to it!

Undoubtedly, many theologians must be charged with responsibility for this sad state of affairs. Some have so emphasized the Three and so vaguely affirmed the One as to invite tritheistic inferences, even though such inferences have been denied.[2] Others have so renounced the sober requirements of reason as to declare the Three and the One beyond all understanding and hence beyond the principle of consistency.

If I believed that Trinitarian doctrine essentially meant what such interpreters have declared, I should have nothing to say for it. Tritheism is unchristian and indefensible, and a doctrine that divides the Godhead into three distinct, concrete Persons, united only by their sharing an abstract divinity and by a unique harmony of will, is essentially tritheistic. If the Three and One were literally beyond understanding and hence beyond the most basic requirements of logic, then they would be to us only syllables signifying nothing. Communication consisting of words without understanding is no communication. Before total mystery, silence would be more fitting than polysyllabic but senseless verbiage.

Actually, I am confident that the doctrine of the Trinity is to be properly understood neither as a veiled, ambiguous tritheism nor as irrational mystery-mongering. If its true significance is to be understood in our day, however, we must look beyond the ponderous and dated terms of Greek metaphysics to the flaming testimony of the Scriptures and of historical experience in the Christian community.

" THE FATHER ALMIGHTY "

Long before the earthly ministry of our Lord, the Hebrews saw that God had revealed himself by creating the heavens and the earth, the varied life of earth and man himself. Again and again this theme is repeated throughout the Old and New Testaments. God has communicated with man through his creation. He has left his mark upon the things that he has made. His earliest form of revelation to his creature, man, was by the very act of making man and his natural environment.

As God showed his ancient children that he was their Creator, he showed also that he was Lawgiver and Judge. Moses and other Hebrews of old learned that men could not make their own rules to suit their convenience or fancy. God covenanted with man in the very act of creation. He has renewed the covenant on many later occasions. The understanding of this covenantal relationship came to the Hebrews through their deliverance from Egypt and their subsequent national experience. Yet they saw in the later pre-Christian centuries that actually God had been covenanting with men long before Moses. He had made a covenant to take his human children to their rightful goal, the Promised Land, if they would live by his Law.

Paul acknowledged, in the second chapter of Romans, that others, outside the reach of the Mosaic law, also knew the law of God and so were answerable to him as their Judge. Through his creation and through his declaration in our experience of his judgments, God has revealed himself as the One who reigns over all that exists. He has warned that we disobey him to our infinite peril. His sovereignty is also evident in all the appearances of his might in the wonderful phenomena of nature around us. The last chapters in The Book of Job bear especially eloquent witness to this revelation of the Sovereign God in nature.

In these ways we know God the Father. If we knew him only through his creation and his righteous sovereignty over the world, it might not occur to us to call him Father. Nevertheless, it is precisely as revealed to us in these acts of communication as Sovereign that God is historically known to the Christian church as God the Father. Thus the Apostles' Creed declares, " I believe in God the Father Almighty, Maker of heaven and earth." Later it speaks of Christ's sitting " on the right hand of God the Father Almighty," a clear reference to God as enthroned Sovereign over all.

The Eternal Son

Long before Jesus was born, the Hebrews had accepted the revelation of God as Creator and Sovereign Lord of all. But now there came a wonderful new revelation of his glory in Jesus Christ. This revelation was, as the Christians called it, " good news." It was good news of God. As God was seen at work in Jesus, he was self-giving, illuminating, healing, saving Love.

But the revelation in Jesus was not only comforting good news. It was also challenge and judgment. The life of Jesus showed what a man could be and should be, even within the ambiguities and perils of human history. By this life of self-giving love God both called men to their rightful destiny and also judged their failures. *Such* judgment had never before been known on earth. In Jesus Christ was the most exacting norm, hence the severest judgment; yet it was the judgment of love, and in this judgment were given also hope, forgiveness, and salvation.

When God was known through Christ, the early believers recognized that this God of self-giving love, humbled and forgiving among men, was wonderfully new, and yet had been with them through the centuries. Through the prophets, indeed, he had been preparing for this climactic self-disclosure in Jesus. He who now showed himself so wonderfully in Jesus had been eternally. Even the creation was now seen anew, as illuminated by this Word made flesh as man. Nothing had been made without the participation of this purposive will now manifest in the self-giving Christ. (John, ch. 1.)

Was this, then, a new God, now known in Christ, a God who should displace Yahweh in the reverent allegiance and obedience of righteous men? The early Christians were generally saved from such an inference by two facts: First, their conviction of the reality and worthiness of Yahweh was too strong to permit his denial, for many of them had been devout Jews before they were Christians and most of the others in the first generation were probably " Godfearing " people already instructed in the basic Jewish beliefs. Secondly, the Old Testament had so well prepared for the coming of

Christ that there was no sharp discontinuity between the understanding of God taught by Jeremiah, Deutero-Isaiah, or the finer psalms and the knowledge of God through Jesus Christ. Hence the answer was given that this was the same God known of old to the Hebrews. Yet the communication of God in his Word made flesh was certainly new, and God as known in Christ was personal, condescending, and subject to the perils and evils of human history, as God had never been known before. Thereafter, to think of God was to think of him as long understood and worshiped but also as now known anew. God was two, and yet the Christians affirmed the two were truly one.

THE HOLY SPIRIT

Moreover, after the postresurrection appearances ceased and Jesus was seen no more among men, the new outpouring of the Holy Spirit brought another new acquaintance with God. To be sure, the Spirit had spoken to prophets of old and was not a stranger to any persons familiar with Old Testament religion. But this Pentecostal Holy Spirit represented God as known in Jesus Christ as well as God the Father known from ancient times. The Holy Spirit came upon the disciples with power, new not only in extent and intensity but also in the kind of effects produced. Not only did the Holy Spirit enable the Christian recipients to speak with amazing courage and effectiveness and to heal the sick, but forged into one united company of faith and love people formerly divided by the most formidable barriers of class, nation, language, and race. This revelation combined continuity with marvelous, life-transforming newness. At first, as the Pauline letters show, there was uncertainty whether God as known in these new manifestations should be spoken of as " the Holy Spirit," " Christ," " the Spirit of Christ " or " the Lord." Indeed, once Paul explicitly states, " The Lord is the Spirit " (II Cor. 3:17).

Eventually, the Holy Spirit was recognized both as a third mode of God's self-disclosure and as God revealed in this self-disclosure. Now God was known as three and yet as one, and all three manifestations of God were regarded as so faithfully revealing his true nature that the threeness was referred to his very being as well as to his self-disclosures. Since each of the " three " was truly God himself and he was one, none could be thought of as subordinate to the others.

The doctrine of the Trinity was at first, then, a testimony to the history of God's revealing of himself to men. Later, the threefold testimony was crystallized in the forms provided by speculative Greek metaphysics. The doctrine did not arise from an effort to represent God as both transcendent, aloof from history, and also involved in history. It arose from the history of the revealing involvement itself. The various philosophical efforts to demonstrate some metaphysical necessity of Trinitarian doctrine are beside the point. So also are efforts to find parallels between the Christian Trinitarian doctrine and the teachings of various non-Christian religions. The Christian doctrine of the Trinity did not arise by abstract inference from some sort of universal religious need observed in human nature or from any kind of metaphysical speculation. It arose in the historical revelation of a profoundly historical faith. Having so arisen in living testimony, it was crystallized in metaphysical forms that have both aided in perpetuating its essentials and also produced in many minds confusion concerning its origin and its highest significance.

PRESENT PRACTICAL RELIGIOUS SIGNIFICANCE

The doctrine of the Trinity has aided immeasurably in preserving the rich complexity of the Christian revelation of God. It is difficult, if not impossible, for one man at one time to hold this whole complex of meaning in balanced comprehension. But so long as the doctrine of the Trinity is maintained, it continues to correct narrow and one-sided views by reminding the church of the whole threefold historical revelation of God.

Walter Marshall Horton remarks acutely that

> " it is impressive that Unitarian thought has, so to speak, been forced by the complexity of the Christian idea of God to run through all three Persons of the Trinity successively in consequence of its refusal to assert them simultaneously." [3]

He illustrates this point by commenting on the actual history of Anglo-American Unitarianism. Rising under the influence of eighteenth-century rationalism, it tended at first to stress the transcendent Creator, the Father conceived in almost deistic terms. Then, in New England Transcendentalism, it became immanentist, stressing the spiritual presence of God in human life and in nature. After that many Unitarians rejected theistic categories altogether and exalted an idealized humanity into deity.[4]

It should be noted, however, that each of these three emphases falls far short of Christian teaching concerning the corresponding mode of the Trinity. God the Father is much more involved in loving concern for men and much more an active agent in history'than the transcendent deity was described to be by the eighteenth-century deists. The spiritual immanence taught by the Concord Transcendentalists was much less personal, specific, and dynamic than the indwelling of the Holy Spirit attested by Christians from Pentecost to the present day. The deification of a general, idealized humanity in modern humanism is far from the doctrine that in one man, Jesus Christ, God was reconciling the world of sinful men to himself.

In short, this one-at-a-time Trinitarianism not only misses the richness of a simultaneous affirmation of Father, Son, and Holy Spirit, but also immeasurably attenuates the meaning of the one mode of God's revelation and being partially affirmed at any given time.

In relation to the various one-sided emphases in contemporary theology, particularly, the insistence that God is the Father and Son and Holy Spirit, should help to restore a sounder perspective. We may illustrate by showing in turn how the affirmation of faith in each of the modes corrects certain recent theological trends.

A strong emphasis upon " God the Father Almighty, Maker of heaven and earth " serves to correct the narrow isolationism of those Christians who insist that the only revelation of God to men is the revelation in Jesus Christ. To know God as Father is to open " the book of nature " with expectancy, appreciation, and reverence comparable to that found expressed in Ps. 104 or in Job, chs. 37 to 41. Before such knowledge the obscurantism of Pentecostal sects and all vague mysticisms are, alike, challenged. It enables the scientist to find his laboratory a holy place and the farmer to see his fields as a temple of God. Knowing that God is the Father, the Christian is reminded that he has " made from one every nation of men . . . that they should seek God " (Acts 17:26-27).

The affirmation of faith in the Father rebukes also any tendency we may feel toward an easygoing moral relativism or superficial sentimentality. One man's opinion is not so good as another's. All does not depend on one's point of view. There is one eternal point of view that is God's, and all men and all opinions stand under his judgment. " It is he that made us, and we are his." (Ps 100:3.) Living and thinking in any way but that for which he made us, we run into increasing estrangement from our neighbors and ourselves. We are children of our Father, and his judgments speak within our very nature, in history, and beyond history.

We know God also as the Son, manifest in Jesus Christ, deeply involved in human affairs and suffering on our behalf. Acknowledgment of the Son corrects barren deistic notions of an aloof God withdrawn from his creation and unconcerned with our misfortune, sin, and peril. Acceptance of the Son undergirds acceptance of the Father as truly Father and not a speculative abstraction nor an unconcerned, absentee potentate.

The doctrine of the Son likewise challenges all such vague mysticisms as neglect ethical demands or even profess to rise above moral distinctions. God as manifest in Jesus is to us the most winsome yet exacting moral norm. If we acknowledge that God *is* uniquely manifest in Jesus, we dare not thereafter evade the rigorous judgment upon us of that historical life.

Moreover, if we truly accept this, that the man Jesus is the Word of God made flesh, then we are not free to degrade man. The doctrine of the Son rebukes reductionist anthropologies that would describe man as a mere animal with oversized brain and conveniently opposing digits, or as a mere battleground of irrational impulses. It stands opposed also to the unrelieved disparagement of man's earthly life in some recent theological utterances.[5] It was precisely in this present earthly life that God manifested himself in the form of man. Moreover, this man Jesus spoke such hopeful words as these to living persons: " Your sins are forgiven you " (Luke 5:20); " Go,

and do not sin again " (John 8:11). In him the writer of the Fourth
Gospel found assurance expressed in the words, " He who believes
in me will also do the works that I do; and greater works than these
will he do " (John 14:12).

Finally, the emphasis on Jesus Christ as "Word made flesh"
serves to correct the teaching and practice of some sects that seem
preoccupied with the seeking of "power from on high" and dramatic "manifestations of the Spirit." In such groups there may be
little concern for the steadfast work and loving service to which
Christ calls his disciples. Stress on the Holy Spirit to the neglect of
Christ tends toward a formless dynamism, with emotional excesses
and little moral growth.

On the other hand, the doctrine of the Holy Spirit is needed as
much in current theology as in any period of Christian history. The
neo-Calvinist emphasis on the transcendence of God, with frequent
denials of the divine immanence, has led to an almost deistic conception of the vast gulf between man and the " wholly other " God.
This trend has been encouraged and augmented by the Kierke-
gaardian teaching of an "infinite qualitative distinction" between
time and eternity. There results a sense of cosmic human loneliness,
a loneliness but slightly relieved by the belief that a hidden God
still lives, in splendid isolation from his children, and that he will,
in his own good time, accomplish his purpose. It is held that once
God broke this cosmic silence to speak his redeeming Word in Jesus
Christ. Some day Christ will come again to make his victory manifest. But we live now "between the times." In this lonely present
we must live by looking back to the first century and forward to
the unknown day of ultimate victory.

Such doctrine comes near to being a unitarianism of the second
mode, though there are suggestions of a binitarian view. Those who
hold it have lost the real meaning of the doctrine of the Holy Spirit
— despite lip service. Hence there is derogatory comment about " religious experience," and there continues an air of pious, detached
cynicism in relation to the present time with all its urgent issues.
Karl Barth, who has done so much to further such views, escapes
the worst practical effects. All through the years he has continued to
issue pronouncements on issues of the day, though his theological

stance has made difficult or impossible any real co-operative communication with him on current issues by other Christian leaders.
On the other hand, many young ministers influenced by him are ex-
cusing their cowardice and laziness on the ground that there is nothing to be done of importance until God speaks again or until Christ
returns. This enables them to join all the cynics and pessimists in
shaking their heads over the sad plight of the world while compla-
cently enjoying life with their families.[6]

All such Christian believers need to be reminded that the Holy
Spirit is in our midst, that the infinite resources of God are available in this present time, so that only wills rejecting him can pre-
vent his will from being done among us. The darkness that hangs
over our world is not due to Christ's having gone away for the time
" between the times." It is due to our little faith, our selfishness, our
provinciality. Pious words about a " coming again " will not save us.
By repentance and the yielding of our wills to his we can even now
experience the presence and power of the Holy Spirit transforming
our lives and our world.

The doctrine of the Holy Spirit is also a beacon light to guide us
out of static or reactionary conservatism. The Holy Spirit offers continuing new revelation of truth. Movements " back to Wesley,"
" back to Luther," or " back to the Reformation " are unworthy of
Christians who believe in the Holy Spirit. We were not called to
make our lives monuments to past heroes of the faith, but living
temples of the Holy Spirit who empowers and leads God's people
today. It would be intolerable for any Christian to accept the obligation today to defend all the doctrines and practices of a Reformer
of the sixteenth or eighteenth century. Such a commitment would
be a present denial of the very spirit that made them Reformers in
their own day — but even more a denial of the Holy Spirit who led
them and is ready now to lead us into truth and practice peculiarly
relevant to our own age.

The Unity of God in the Three Modes

In all three modes of his revelation, all faithfully representing his
very being, God has shown himself to be one. Paul, writing to the
Corinthians about the nonexistence of idols, quotes from the Shema

the words, "There is no God but one" (I Cor. 8:4), and in a following sentence declares that

> "for us there is one God, the Father, from whom are all things and for whom we exist, and one Lord, Jesus Christ, through whom are all things and through whom we exist" (v. 6).

Likewise, he writes in the same letter,

> "Now there are varieties of gifts, but the same Spirit; and there are varieties of service, but the same Lord; and there are varieties of working, but it is the same God who inspires them all in every one" (ch. 12:4-6).

Again he writes, "For by one Spirit we were all baptized into one body" (v. 13).

The three modes of God's being, as revealed to us, are all modes of one God. He is one more profoundly than he is three. Moreover, in all the three modes of his self-disclosure he shows himself to be a personal God, who knows all things and acts with purpose. In all three modes he is revealed as trustworthy, supremely faithful, and steadfast in all his ways. In all three modes he discloses also his freedom to act creatively and particularly in our behalf. In all three modes he declares his love for us. In each of the three modes he is holy, the supreme Deity before whose presence we bow in awe. In his holiness is much of mystery, and it could not be otherwise. In all existence there is much that is mysterious to our limited understanding. How much more in God, Maker of all things!

Even the three modes of his being disclosed by the threefold historic revelation partake of this mystery in their tri-unity. When we have said all that we can to make clear the grounds and meaning of our affirmation that God is the Trinity, we must yet wait in silence before the mystery that remains. It is important that we speak with all the rational clarity possible. But in the presence of God the Father, Son, and Holy Spirit, it is even more important that, having spoken, we be silent. Understanding must finally give way to adoration in which all words fail.

VI.

Man as Divinely Confronted

IN GOD'S PURPOSE

The most important truth about man is that he is created by God for a divinely purposed destiny. Some Christians are denying that this is of first importance. They say the most important truth is that man is a sinner. But this is a serious distortion of Biblical teaching and of logical relations. Sin has no meaning apart from some high expectation or norm of conduct and being.

The Greek usage in the New Testament is instructive. The common word for sin, *hamartia,* signifies a missing of the target and hence a failure to gain one's share of the prize. It is evident that if one were not offered a prize for hitting a prescribed target, there could be no such failure. Where there is no target, there is no missing the target. Even the other words occasionally used to connote sin have similar implications. Thus *opheilēmata* (debts) depend for their very existence on a prior contract or positive transaction in relation to which debts can be incurred. Finally, *paraptōmata* (trespasses) means literally a falling or slipping to the side, a deviation from the proper path. Obviously, there must be a path one is supposed to follow before one can deviate from it.

Actually, the conception of sin, both in the Old Testament and in the New, presupposes a covenantal relation between God and man. After the deliverance of Israel from Egypt and the acceptance by the nation of a covenantal obligation to God, the prophets taught that God had much earlier covenanted with Abraham and even with Noah and Adam. By the creation itself God placed men under covenantal bonds with him. The New Testament (or more accurately New Covenant) represents the work of Christ as fulfilling the old covenant and as inaugurating the new covenant. (Cf. I Cor. 6:20; 7:22.) A positive relation to God's purpose is chronologically and logically prior to sin, under either covenant.

Other views of man are widely held in the twentieth century. He is sometimes regarded as a curiously mutated mammal or as a machine governed by an extraordinarily complex control box, or, again, as a mass of striving, irrational drives. On any such essentially reductionist or depersonalized view of man there is no meaning to be assigned to such terms as *sin,* while *salvation* could at best imply a preservation of the individual or species despite some threatening peril.

It is only when man is viewed in a relation above the level of his mere present existence that *sin* or *salvation from sin* can have meaning. A machine, a mammal, or a mere psychic complex, as such, does not sin. The very possibility of man's sinning is due to his standing in relation to God, his Creator and Judge. God has fitted him for a destiny that he purposes to give him. Sin is estrangement from God and from the divinely purposed human destiny. Hence, in sinning man becomes estranged also from his own true self. He is created in dependence upon God, and any disturbance of this relation produces a sense of alienation in the depths of his own being.

We see in Christ what God purposed that we should be. He is God's creative purpose for man made flesh. Christ is the reason for our existence. What we see in Christ is a will perfected in love, purity, and courage. But above all we see in him the relationship for which we were created — a relationship of intimate, understanding love and obedient trust in God.

SINNER

In all ages there is remarkable agreement among men that something is wrong with their condition. Biologically the human race has done very well, indeed, spreading over most of the earth's land area, beating many natural enemies, and, in the last centuries especially, increasing very rapidly in numbers. Yet this biological success has little influence on the deep discontent with which man is afflicted. Everywhere men are anxious and feel that somehow they have missed the way. Sometimes they blame outward circumstances, political mistakes, foreign foes, troublesome demons, angry ancestral spirits, or bad luck. Even when projecting their discontent in all such ways they are likely to feel an inner anxiety of guilt and seek some method of changing their relationships in order to make them feel whole and at home.

In the New Testament the word " sin " is often used, especially by Paul, to connote this condition of man interpreted as an estrangement from God, a banishment from his favor, and a bondage to all the powers that oppose him. However, Paul occasionally speaks of " sins," using the plural form to indicate various acts or decisions of will contrary to God's purpose. John also uses " sin " more often in the singular to mean a condition of guilt or a dwelling apart from " the light " or " the truth." On the other hand, in the Synoptic Gospels the noun in the singular is never used except in Matt. 12:31, where the adjective *pasa* has a distributive effect implying a plural number, like the English word " every " in the phrase " every sin." In all three Synoptic Gospels the plural form is used freely.

It is not accurate to say, then, as many recent theologians have said, that the New Testament is concerned with *sin,* a condition, rather than with *sins,* that is, acts or decisions of will contrary to God's will. The New Testament writers are concerned *both* with men's sinful acts and with the condition of the soul that produces such acts and is augmented by such acts. Jesus is represented in the Synoptic Gospels as more concerned about men's *sins,* while John and Paul, showing as they do, more inclination to generalization and abstraction, with more Persian and Greek influence in evidence, speak more of *sin.*

Whether we focus attention at first on sinful acts or on sinful condition, we are bound to ask soon why people whom God has created are so far opposing his will and so seriously lost, and why we find it so easy to sin but so hard to keep in the right way. The traditional Christian doctrine of original sin explains our present condition of guilt and our inclination to sin by referring to the sin of

Adam. The Bible nowhere tells how the guilt or the inclination has been transmitted from Adam to us. Indeed, it is doubtful that the doctrine that *guilt* has been transmitted is taught in the New Testament at all. Paul says that

> "sin came into the world through one man and death through sin, and so death spread to all men *because all men sinned*" (Rom. 5:12; emphasis mine).

Some liberal Christians have taught that each individual came into the world either morally good or morally neutral. But most influential theologians, even among liberals, have interpreted man's condition more grimly than this. For example, Walter Rauschenbusch vigorously defended the doctrine of original sin. He taught the transmission of sinfulness, both by biological propagation and through social tradition, evil institutions, and harmful personal influence.[1] He stated that "evil does flow down the generations through the channels of biological coherence." He went on to explain,

> "Idiocy and feeblemindedness, neurotic disturbances, weakness of inhibition, perverse desires, stubbornness and antisocial impulses in children must have had their adequate biological causes somewhere back on the line, even if we lack the record."[2]

He did not place his major emphasis on biological transmission, however, but rather on social transmission. So he wrote:

> "A theology for the social gospel would have to say that original sin is partly social. It runs down the generations not only by biological propagation but also by social assimilation."[3]

The medieval and Reformational doctrine that human babies are born guilty and condemned by God is unethical, unbiblical, and altogether indefensible. Fortunately, most contemporary Protestant theologians agree in rejecting it. The newborn infant is morally neutral in the sense that he is neither virtuous nor sinful. But this does not imply that he will confront his own moral decisions without weighting or influence on either side. He is not an atomistic individual, deciding in untarnished isolation what he will be and do. By the time he is able to make any kind of meaningful decisions he will have become deeply involved in a world full of fear, hostility, selfishness, and guilt. In many ways these conditions will have made their mark upon him and he will continue to live his life amid the tensions, temptations, and ambiguities which they bring to bear upon him.

There are other factors besides social influence — in the broadest sense — that tend to load the balance against his efforts to live righteously. As Albert C. Knudson pointed out, before the child comes to the age of moral decision he has already formed infantile habits that, though *amoral then,* fasten their bonds upon him and tend strongly to perpetuate themselves after further indulgence in them has become sinful. An example would be the temper tantrum, which is not sinful in the baby, but is sinful in an adult and for some indefinable period of years before adulthood. Likewise, any choice made in error though in good faith may involve us in highly compromising and tempting circumstances or in habits later seen to be evil, but hard to break.

Another important negative influence is the temptation to prideful rebellion inherent in the discovery of personal freedom by a developing finite person. This is one of the insights symbolized in the profoundly searching myth of the Fall in the Garden of Eden.[4]

It must be added that in every situation of choice only the *best* possibility before us is the righteous choice, while any other is evil, just as there is but one correct answer to a problem in multiplication while there are possible wrong answers of infinite number. It is easier to find one of the wrong solutions of a moral problem than to discover and adopt the right solution. Yet any solution other than the best possible, whether willfully wrong or not, involves us in opposition to God's will and adds to our temptation to further sin as well as to other evil consequences.

" In the Image of God "

" So God created man in his own image, in the image of God he created him; male and female he created them." (Gen. 1:27.) So reads the Genesis account of human origins and so the church has taught through the centuries. But what is meant by "the image of God"? How much is it affected by man's sin? Is the ordinary sinful man we see now in the image of God? In what sense?

These questions are not of interest solely to people who assume the literal truth of the ancient account. Many who would either explain away the six "days" of creation and the "Sabbath" rest of Yahweh, or regard these as projecting back into creation the priestly author's interest in the Hebrew Sabbatical tradition, would nevertheless raise in utmost seriousness the questions about the image of God.

Quite apart from the ancient writer, we find in human experience the sense of a high and noble destiny that we should be fulfilling. We could be and rightly are more than we actually show ourselves to be. While living on earth, sharing much of life with the other creatures of earth and being, biologically, mammalian bipeds, we nevertheless know that we are not mere animals and can never be content with living "by bread alone." [5]

Some writers insist that the divine image is present only in man as created in righteousness. Man as he actually is, then, is not regarded as being in the image of God, although in Jesus this image is encountered and the Christian knows it in Jesus alone. Others, like Paul Ramsey, regard the image as implying, not any qualities of human life, but rather a relationship of man to God. As a man's image appears in a mirror when he stands before it, although the mirror is not in the least like a man, so the image of God appears in man's being consciously before God. On this view, "nothing about man not presently involved in response to God can be called God's image." [6] Similar views are to be found in the writings of Karl Barth and Sören Kierkegaard.

Ramsey cites Augustine and Paul, as well as Kierkegaard and Barth, in support of this "relational" view. However, approval by the two ancient interpreters of our faith seems doubtful. To be sure, both Augustine and Paul plainly teach that we come into the fullest likeness to God which he purposes for us only when we are regenerated by him and stand in obedient faith toward him. Surely no Christian should hesitate to agree wholeheartedly with that. God has made us for life in relationship with him and in other relationships under his will. We cannot fulfill our proper destinies apart from him.

Yet both Augustine and Paul affirm also a substantial likeness. Ramsey himself quotes Augustine's words describing man as

> "created after thy image and likeness, in that very image and likeness of thee (that is, the power of reason and understanding) on account of which he was set over all irrational creatures." [7]

Augustine elsewhere stresses the imperfection of this likeness as compared with that to be found in Jesus and teaches that it is sustained only by God, who first gave it. But such teachings do not nullify the substantive character of the divine likeness that Augustine finds in man as the dependent creature of God. Moreover, Augustine's doctrine of love of neighbor is predicated on the discovery that in every neighbor is the likeness of God. Indeed, at times he goes farther and speaks as if the real or potential good in the neighbor were itself God in the neighbor. [8] This identification of goodness, wherever found, with God himself is doubtless due to Augustine's Platonic concretizing of abstract universals. But we can wholly agree with his finding of *likeness* to God in man. [9]

When we turn to the New Testament we find that the "image" or "likeness" is plainly described as being in various degrees of glory. The fullness of the glory of God appears only in the face of Christ. (E.g., see II Cor. 3:18; 4:6; and John 1:14.) The divine likeness in this complete sense is not a present human condition but an eschatological hope. This is the thought expressed in the First Letter of John:

> "Beloved, we are God's children now; it does not yet appear what we shall be, but we know that when he appears we shall be like him, for we shall see him as he is" (ch. 3:2).

On the other hand, in an imperfect degree all men are to be regarded as in the likeness of God. James, condemning evil use of the tongue, complains, "With it we bless the Lord and Father, and with it we curse men, who are made in the likeness of God." [10] So Paul, too, speaking of the Corinthian controversy about head coverings in worship, writes, "For a man ought not to cover his head, since he is the image and glory of God" (I Cor. 11:7). To be sure, according to the customary thought of his day, he goes on to exclude woman from this honored status, in plain distortion of Gen. 1:26-27. But this does not alter the obvious fact that Paul, like James, regards the doctrine of the divine likeness in man as applying to man as he is now. Moreover, he is using the doctrine specifically to condemn a too abject servility in the presence of God. This theme accords with a mood occasionally found in the Old Testament, as, for example, in the word of God to the prostrate Ezekiel: "Son of man, stand upon your feet, and I will speak with you" (Ezek. 2:1).

It may be freely conceded that the New Testament is primarily concerned with the "glory of Christ, who is the likeness of God" (II Cor. 4:4), and with the fulfilling of this likeness in us by God's regenerating grace. At the same time, it is clearly appropriate also, within the context of Biblical language, to speak of men in their present actual existence, as, in a lesser sense, in the image or likeness of God.

When we turn from the question of Biblical language and propriety of expression to the more basic question of real relations, it is much more evident that there is a genuine likeness between human beings and God. Here all that has been said earlier about the personal nature of God is again relevant. If God is aware of events, we are like him in this respect, while presumably stones, trees, electrons, and galaxies are not. To be sure, his awareness must unimaginably transcend our own limited and faltering consciousness. Nevertheless, it is of utmost importance that among all God's creatures that have being without knowing that they are, we are like God in this — that we not only are but we know that we are.[11]

Likewise, our capacity to relate some data to others, the capacity we call the power of reason, is not only matched but infinitely overmatched by the vast systematic relatedness of the processes that constitute our cosmic environment. We have already noted grounds for attributing the complex system of nature to the rational purpose of God the Creator. In this, too, then, we are like him — that he has given us the power to reason and also to plan purposively according to our rational thought. Again, the vast differences of comprehension and power must be granted, and the self-deceiving proclivities of man's thought must be taken into account. There still remains a likeness of high significance between the infinite rational purpose of God and the limited powers of reason and purpose in man.

Closely related to the qualities already mentioned is the morally significant will. In the moral sense, only a personal being can be good or evil, righteous or sinful. Such categories would be meaningless in description of a star or molecule and presumably likewise in evaluation of a rosebush or a lion. Man is aware of good and evil possibilities *as* good and evil. He must choose between them and in choosing is describable in ethical categories. To be sure, Christians regard God as wholly and invariably righteous, faithful to his perfect norms of righteousness as well as to their ultimate source, while men are wavering and ambiguous in their obedience as well as often directly rebellious. But men, like God, live in the dimensions of moral meaning.

Beyond even these important likenesses is the divinely established need of man for positive righteousness, truth, beauty, and holiness — in short, for perfection. In all the scientist's quest of explanation, the artist's longing for aesthetic excellence, the mystic's ecstatic rapture, is exemplified man's need of godlike perfection which can be fulfilled only in God himself. However we may twist and turn, however recklessly we may seek fulfillment of our deepest needs elsewhere, we have been made for communion with God and can be satisfied with nothing less. It is not being contended that actual man is *like* God in needing godlike perfection. This need does show that man fulfills his own nature only by participation with God in His perfection.

It is often asked whether man is naturally good or evil, and this question has been much argued. We must answer that man can be true to his own essential nature only by being good. But this must not lead to the supposition that to be good requires little or no effort, since goodness will come " naturally." On the contrary, to be good is exceedingly difficult, while to be evil, one has only to let his impulses have sway. Man cannot be himself — his true, essential, created self — without the effort of a will transformed and turned beyond himself by the grace of God.

VII.

Justification and Sanctification

The terms of the New Testament translated as "justify" (*dikaioō*) and "justification" (*dikaiōsis*) are closely but somewhat ambiguously related to the word for "righteous" (*dikaios*). To "justify" a person may mean to *make* him righteous or it may mean to *treat* him as righteous, that is, to acquit him.

The terms translated "sanctify" (*hagiazō*) and "sanctification" (*hagiasmos*) are similarly related to one of the words for "sacred" or "holy" (*hagios*), but with less ambiguity. It is true that to "sanctify" may mean to *treat* as holy, but when speaking of human beings, probably no New Testament author ever does employ the word in this sense. Rather, to "sanctify" a person is to *make* him holy, especially, though not solely, in the moral sense.[1] "Sanctification," then, is the process of making holy or the effect of this process, that is, the being made holy.

In precise theological discourse, it has become customary to use the word "justification" to mean the acquittal of a sinful man before God or God's acceptance of a sinful man as if he were righteous, while "sanctification" is employed to mean a change in the actual condition of a man, the purging of sinfulness from his heart and life. Thus, John Wesley wrote,

> "By justification we are saved from the guilt of sin, and restored to the favor of God; by sanctification we are saved from the power and root of sin, and restored to the image of God."[2]

We must raise several important and often controversial questions concerning justification and sanctification. What is the role of man himself in his justification? How are faith and works related? Are justification and sanctification separable in reality or only in thought? Do they occur in various stages or degrees? May they be completed during our present earthly life?

Man's Participation in His Justification

The many exhortations in Christian Scripture and preaching to "repent," "have faith," "believe," or "come to Christ" would seem to imply clearly that there is something that a man must do to be justified. When the jailer at Philippi lay trembling before Paul and Silas and cried out, "Men, what must I do to be saved?" they did not reply that he was saved without doing anything, nor did they rebuke his asking such a question, since God saved whomever he pleased without man's co-operation. No, instead, they replied directly, telling him what he was to do: "Believe in the Lord Jesus, and you will be saved, you and your household" (Acts 16:31). Later we must consider the place assigned to deeds in New Testament teaching concerning salvation. Right now attention is being called to the fact that even those passages which clearly teach justification by faith do not minimize, but rather stress the act of will that a man must perform, namely, the decision of faith in Christ.

Even when Paul writes to the Romans that "a man is justified by faith apart from works of law" (Rom. 3:28), he is writing in utmost earnestness, precisely because their salvation depends on their having faith in God. This, too, is something difficult for sinful man to do — this turning of trust and faithful commitment away from self and all earthly powers to God. Both Luther and Calvin sought to avoid any such conclusion, but with little success. Calvin goes so far as to say,

> "For with respect to justification, faith is a thing merely passive, bringing nothing of our own to conciliate the favor of God, but receiving what we need from Christ." [3]

But he insists that this faith in God must be present if we are to be justified. So long as we trust in any other power we are not open to receive the divine grace.

" But not to dwell any longer on this, we may lay it down as a brief, but general and certain maxim, that he is prepared for a participation of the benefits of divine mercy, who has wholly divested himself, I will not say of his righteousness, which is a mere nullity, but of the vain and airy phantom of righteousness; for as far as any man is satisfied with himself, so far he raises an impediment to the exercise of the grace of God." [4]

It may require considerable self-discipline and much directing of attention to Christian writing or preaching to bring a person to such self-abnegation. This is precisely the reason why Calvin wrote and preached so strenuously of its necessity.[5]

We have confronted the question of man's participation only in relation to thoroughgoing doctrines of salvation by faith alone. There is in the New Testament much teaching that gives to man's will a larger role than such doctrines are usually understood to admit. To notice such teaching will carry us into study of the relation between faith and works in our salvation.

Before we leave the doctrine of justification by faith alone, we must observe important truth in this teaching of the Reformation — and, indeed, of the classical Christian tradition, both Catholic and Protestant.

All our hope is in God. We have no ground of hope whatsoever in ourselves apart from his prior initiative and his forgiving love. Our very existence is dependent upon his grace. Our hope of fulfilling both his purpose and our own essential nature depends upon our turning to him in voluntary, grateful reception of his renewing love. Even this turning to him requires prior action moving from him to us, awakening our insight into our own guilt and need, and stirring our hope in him. This divine initiative was taken in Jesus Christ. The action of God taken in Christ has been transmitted by the continuing work of the Holy Spirit in the human community of faith (the living church) to the present time. As this community of forgiveness touches the individual, God, working through and beside this fellowship, generates in the sinner the beginning of contrition and of hope. In this way there is created for the sinful man the possibility of faith. The man then confronts the crisis, the parting of the ways, and he must choose. He may turn from the light offered to him and return into darkness. On the other hand, he may move, by repentance, faith, and gratitude, into the light of God's grace and so be justified.

If a man does turn in faith to accept God's gift, this does not mean that he thus earns the right to receive God's mercy. Faith does not *merit* the gift, else it would not be a gift. Faith does *receive* the gift, freely given by the grace of God.

FAITH AND WORKS

There is much emphasis in the New Testament on the necessity of good deeds as required for our salvation. This emphasis is especially prominent in the accounts of Jesus' teachings in the Synoptic Gospels. An especially well-known contemporary Calvinist is quoted as confessing that he " found the Synoptics regrettably Pelagian."

Toward the end of the Sermon on the Mount, preoccupied as it is with the deeds and attitudes required of all who are to be in the Kingdom of God, Jesus says:

"Not every one who says to me, 'Lord, Lord,' shall enter the kingdom of heaven, but he who does the will of my Father who is in heaven. . . .
"Every one then who hears these words of mine and does them will be like a wise man who built his house upon the rock. . . . And every one who hears these words of mine and does not do them will be like a foolish man who built his house upon the sand." (Matt. 7:21, 24, 26.)

Especially emphatic and concrete is the stress on works in Jesus' familiar and well-loved parable of the last judgment (ch. 25:31-46). Here Jesus pictures all the peoples of the world gathered before the heavenly " Son of man," the " King," for judgment. Some are sent to his right hand, and the King says to them, " Come, O blessed of my Father, inherit the kingdom prepared for you from the foundation of the world." To the others, placed on the left, he says, " Depart from me, you cursed, into the eternal fire prepared for the devil and his angels." And what is the basis of division? Is it an affirmation of belief or trust? Is it even a personal commitment to Christ? No, it is simply the having done or having failed to do deeds of kindness for other people. The blessed people on the right have fed the hungry, given drink to the thirsty, welcomed the stranger, clothed the naked, visited the sick and the imprisoned. The condemned people on the left have not done these things. That is all.

This teaching is best viewed as a parable rather than a description of the actual final judgment to be. The teaching regarding " eternal fire " and " eternal punishment " does not appear in the earlier Pauline letters and is not unambiguously presented in Mark, the earliest of the Gospels. Jesus' own literal belief in eternal fiery torment for the condemned is in serious doubt.[6] Moreover, if taken literally, this passage would imply both the salvation and the damnation of most people, since most human beings have sometimes ministered to the needy and sometimes lamentably failed to do so. Yet the central teaching remains crystal clear. God approves and blesses kind deeds; he despises and condemns coldhearted indifference.

The amount of explicit ethical teaching in the Gospel of John is surprisingly small as compared with that in the other Gospels. Yet John makes deeds the test of that love which is all-important for our salvation. Quite unequivocally we read:

> " If you love me, you will keep my commandments. . . . He who has my commandments and keeps them, he it is who loves me; and he who loves me will be loved by my Father, and I will love him and manifest myself to him." (John 14:15, 21.)

The Letter of James not only emphasizes works, as do the Synoptic Gospels, but places the requirement of works in direct and explicit contrast to an antinomian doctrine of salvation by faith alone. It is James who exhorts his readers:

> " But be doers of the word, and not hearers only, deceiving yourselves. . . . But he who looks into the perfect law, the law of liberty, and perseveres, being no hearer that forgets but a doer that acts, he shall be blessed in his doing. . . . Religion that is pure and undefiled before God and the Father is this: to visit orphans

and widows in their affliction, and to keep oneself unstained from the world." (Ch. 1:22, 25, 27.)

More explicitly he confronts antinomian claims of faith in biting satire:

"What does it profit, my brethren, if a man says he has faith but has not works? Can his faith save him? If a brother or sister is ill-clad and in lack of daily food, and one of you says to them, 'Go in peace, be warmed and filled,' without giving them the things needed for the body, what does it profit? So faith by itself, if it has no works, is dead." (Ch. 2:14-17.)

Observing such teachings, some liberals have concluded that the doctrine of salvation by faith in Christ was a Pauline perversion of the true gospel. So one hears the optimistic and activistic Jesus contrasted with the dour and misanthropic Paul or the "religion of Jesus" set over against the "religion about Jesus."

Such an inference does justice neither to Jesus nor to Paul. In the first place, it assumes that we have the firsthand teachings of Jesus in the Synoptic Gospels and only the teachings of Paul in the Pauline letters. Actually, of course, the letters were written first and the Gospels are testimonies of faith already influenced by Paul, so that it is exceedingly difficult to disentangle Jesus' own teachings from the witness of his disciples to their faith in him, a faith that is bound to have colored their memory and report of his teachings.

Moreover, the Synoptic Gospels contain much teaching about salvation by faith, and Paul strongly emphasizes the necessity of upright life and generous deeds in terms reflecting the same source as the sayings of Jesus reported in the earlier Gospels.

In the Synoptic Gospels many accounts of healings by Jesus emphasize the faith that made them possible, and there is much evidence that the healings were regarded as symbolic of salvation. In the Marcan account of his home-coming it is clearly implied that Jesus was unable to perform many miracles among his old neighbors at Nazareth "because of their unbelief" (Mark 6:5-6). Frequently, he is reported to have praised faith and rebuked lack of faith. The acts commanded by him are often acts that would require the decisive commitment of faith — as fishermen leaving their nets to follow him, a rich young man giving all he possessed to the poor and then, penniless, following Jesus, or the disciples performing deeds of kindness in the " name " of Jesus. (E.g., see Mark 9:37.)

Those who find a contrast between the teachings of Jesus and Paul often point out that Jesus enjoins faith in God whereas Paul calls for faith in Jesus Christ. When the different situations are taken into account, the difference fades. People who have come to Jesus for help scarcely need to be exhorted to look to Jesus. Jesus acts as mediator, directing their faith to God. Since Paul too has found his new faith in God through Christ, he directs others to Christ as the great mediator of God's forgiving grace.

Justification and Sanctification Inseparable

When reading Paul's strictures on " works " we need to observe that he contrasts faith not with good deeds but with " works of the law," that is, efforts to please God by fulfilling the elaborate casuistry of Jewish law. At the same time, he devotes much attention to the ethical requirements of faith. Faith does not free us from ethical requirements. Rather, the grace of God given through Christ and received by faith enables us to live righteously, as Paul had found he could not do without this work of Christ. Justification by faith is not a substitute for sanctification. The two are inseparable.

For example, Paul writes:

> " Are we to sin because we are not under law but under grace? By no means! Do you not know that if you yield yourselves to any one as obedient slaves, you are slaves of the one whom you obey, either of sin, wh:ch leads to death, or of obedience, which leads to righteousness? . . . For just as you once yielded your members to impurity and to greater and greater iniquity, so now yield your members to righteousness for sanctification.
>
> " When you were slaves of sin, you were free in regard to righteousness. But then what return did you get from the things of which you are now ashamed? The end of those things is death. But now that you have been set free from sin and have become slaves of God, the return you get is sanctification and its end, eternal life." (Rom. 6:15-16, 19b-22.)

There has always been a temptation for Christians to seek a divorce between justification and sanctification, which God has joined together inseparably. It is so easy to sing "Jesus paid it all" and forget that even in that rather unsatisfactory gospel song the next words are "All to him I owe." So persistent is the hold of sin upon us that we want the comfort, security, and joy of being Christians without living like Christians. Apparently some Christians of the first century succumbed to this temptation, and this was precisely why James had to make such a vigorous attack on the teaching that men could be saved by faith while continuing to live undisciplined lives of sin. James was no more opposed to the doctrine of justification by faith than Paul was opposed to deeds of faith. James provides a platform on which Paul, too, could stand, in the following passage:

> "But some one will say, 'You have faith and I have works.' Show me your faith apart from your works, and I by my works will show you my faith. . . . Was not Abraham our father justified by works, when he offered his son Isaac upon the altar? You see that faith was active along with his works, and faith was completed by works. . . . For as the body apart from the spirit is dead, so faith apart from works is dead." (James 2:18, 21-22, 26.)

With this may be compared Paul's statement:

> "Do you not know that the unrighteous will not inherit the kingdom of God? Do not be deceived; neither the immoral, nor idolaters, nor adulterers, nor homosexuals, nor thieves, nor the greedy, nor drunkards, nor revilers, nor robbers will inherit the kingdom of God. And such were some of you. But you were washed, you were sanctified, you were justified in the name of the Lord Jesus Christ and in the Spirit of our God." (I Cor. 6:9-11.)

Concerning the definition of justification and sanctification and the general understanding of their relationship, I believe that John Wesley faithfully represented New Testament teaching. In definition of justification he wrote, "Justification is another word for pardon."[7] Defining the two terms together, he said,

" By justification we are saved from the guilt of sin, and restored to the favour of God; by sanctification we are saved from
the power and root of sin, and restored to the image of God." [8]

I should want to add the interpretation that this restoration is relative, since the likeness to God was not wholly absent before the
sanctification nor is the likeness of man to God ever made complete.

Concerning the temporal relation of justification Wesley wrote,
" And at the same time that we are justified, yea, in that very moment, sanctification begins." [9] How could it be otherwise? Justification by faith requires repentance in faith. This implies a reorienta-
tion of life toward God in humble and grateful obedience. God's
pardon breaking through man's despair, cynicism, pride, or indifference — or all of these — opens the human heart to receive his
grace by which the will is turned from evil to good. This does not
assure a man of perpetual sinlessness. It does assure him of a decisive victory over sin. Subsequently both the justification and sanctification must be renewed ever and again. For we stand in the need
of God's continuing forgiveness, and whenever aware of our sin
we must seek his pardon anew. We live by his grace in all our quest
for completion of our sanctification.

The references to Wesley raise the question how far sanctification
may be carried in this life. Wesley and all his less optimistic critics
would be agreed that never in this life is any man brought to such
perfection as would mean the end of all quest for more complete
conformity to God's will. The " Christian perfection " or " entire
sanctification " for which Wesley holds out hope and exhorts aspiration does not imply absence of ignorance, error, temptation, or need
of further forgiveness. It means simply an uninterrupted *intent* to
obey God's will. The lack of perfect conformity to God's will in
such a state is due to honest error or to lack of genuine freedom to
obey. Such lack does not gainsay a man's " Christian perfection."
But the " entirely sanctified " person does not indulge a rebellious
will or voluntarily yield himself to unholy passions. One mark of
his " entire sanctification " is his continual reliance on God's forgiving love and his constant aspiration to become more like Christ. [10]

The recent developments of depth psychology have undoubtedly made more complicated the questions that Wesley faced in framing his doctrine of Christian perfection. We have been made increasingly aware of the human capacities and resourcefulness in self-deception. We know that a person's conscious intent may be excellent, and yet his action and even the form given his conscious thought may be controlled by subconscious motives that he would consciously despise. The modern evidences of such ambiguities and self-deceptions make us less hopeful than Wesley that " the very root of sin " in us will be completely removed in this life, or that we have the power accurately to appraise our own freedom from sinful motives.

However, we ought still to learn from Wesley — who learned from Paul and Jesus — that we should be satisfied with nothing less than entire sanctification of our lives in the likeness of Christ. Nor should we conclude that it is beyond the power of God's grace to make " perfect in love " persons who steadfastly seek his forgiveness and strength.

This emphasis of John Wesley is urgently needed today — for the same reason that it was so needed in eighteenth-century England. By and large the theology and preaching of the day have come to easy terms with the half-Christian and unchristian standards prevalent in our society. To be sure, as Paul L. Holmer, a frequent critic of liberal theology, says of recent neo-orthodoxy, " In the preaching of the post-Niebuhrians we get a lot of vicarious groaning and lamentation for the entire nation." [11] But this has become the conventional, accepted posture of theologians and up-to-date preachers, and it does not bother us much.

> " Theological conclusions about the guilt of us all are a lot easier to assimilate and use than is the first-person-singular sense of guilt." [12]

Holmer is precisely accurate when he describes some preaching that is produced by neo-orthodox theology:

> " Most of the preaching I hear confirms me in my ethical mediocrity and even counsels a kind of good citizenship in this earthly kingdom. The vogue is to infer that because human history and

nature are what they are, the quest for perfection commanded by Jesus ought not to be pursued." [18]

It is precisely " the quest for perfection commanded by Jesus " that ought to be pursued by the Christian. To refuse to pursue it, whether on the ostensible grounds of an accommodationist liberalism or a hand-wringing neo-orthodoxy, is to turn from Christ and put one's faith in the world.

Our quest for entire sanctification should be carried on without that subjective preoccupation with our own feelings or even our own religious experience in the best sense which has often bedeviled earnest people of the pietistic tradition. The more mature levels of spiritual life require the centering of attention primarily upon God and secondarily upon tasks to be performed in responsibility to him. Only occasionally should we engage in self-examination, and then should employ principally the more objective norms of Christlike conduct and attitudes toward other persons while seeking God's grace the better to serve the needs of our neighbors and communities. Otherwise we invite self-deception, spiritual pride, a faith fluctuating with our variable emotional states, and the deadly peril of self-centered disillusionment. Our hope is in God and we are to pray first that his " kingdom come " and his " will be done, on earth as it is in heaven." Nevertheless, to pray that prayer in faith is to pray for perfection in obedient love, beginning with oneself.

PART THREE

THE PEOPLE OF GOD

VIII.

The Christian Life

THE ETHICAL TEACHING OF JESUS

As the Synoptic Gospels report to us the teachings of our Lord, these teachings are readily understood in a legalistic sense. Jesus speaks again and again in the imperative mood. Do not these commandments of his constitute a new system of law, from which more detailed inferences are to be made, thus providing a whole system of Christian casuistry to take the place of the old Jewish law?

Roman Catholic ethics has been highly developed along these lines, though using other sources in addition to the teachings of Jesus. The vast system of canon law provides rules for the greatest variety of circumstances. There are few crimes too grave to be capable of defense by a skilled lawyer armed with this system; there are few acts so innocent as to be incapable of condemnation by appeal to the same law. With heavy heart one observes the burden that this Roman casuistry lays upon the conscience of the people, as, for example, when the most notoriously adulterous couple, with wealth and fame, are publicly married by a prominent bishop with the blessing of the Vatican, while many another man and woman, of unblemished reputation, are publicly denounced as adulterous by high officials of the church, simply because their marriage vows are taken before a minister of their non-Roman Christian faith. In the face of such monstrous law our thoughts are turned to Jesus' words:

" Woe to you lawyers also! for you load men with burdens hard to bear, and you yourselves do not touch the burdens with one of your fingers." [1]

Generally less onerous, but also a betrayal of Christian freedom, are petty Protestant sectarian rules like that which forbids buttons on clothing, as vain show, while permitting luxurious and expensive automobiles, because the founding fathers made no rules about the then nonexistent motor cars. Again, several Protestant churches forbid the marriage of divorced persons, while having no official statement about any other moral or spiritual prerequisite of Christian marriage. As if the only people unprepared for such marriage were persons already divorced! Attempts to establish Christian standards of life by rules are hardly more successful today than among the ancient Galatians whom Paul chided for so quickly forsaking the freedom of faith to submit again to the bonds of the law. (Cf. especially Gal. 3:1 to 5:12.)

It should be clear to the discerning reader that the concrete injunctions given by Jesus, for example, in the Sermon on the Mount, were intended not as statements of rules but as illustrating and symbolizing a spirit in which life was to be lived. When he spoke sharply of a man's anger toward his brother (Matt. 5:22), he did not outlaw every instance of anger. He himself was angry on occasion. (Cf. Mark 3:5; Matt. 23:13-33.) He did enjoin patience, mercy, and self-control.

When Jesus says, " Give to him who begs from you, and do not refuse him who would borrow from you " (Matt. 5:42), he does not lay down a law for the treatment of every drunken beggar wanting money for another drink, nor of every swindler who wants to borrow money with which he intends to abscond. He is graphically teaching a generous spirit and conduct appropriate to kindly concern for others. When he teaches the turning of the other cheek and the giving of both coat and cloak when you have been sued for your coat (vs. 39-40), he is not laying down a law for every occasion, regardless of the public good. He is teaching the eager search for ways of disarming hostility with patient long-suffering and positive, generous good will.

He says,

> " But when you pray, go into your room and shut the door and pray to your Father who is in secret; and your Father who sees in secret will reward you " (ch. 6:6).

Does he, then, as some Christians have supposed, condemn congregational worship and all public prayer? His customary attendance in the services of the synagogue and his reported prayers in the presence of others make answer. He is enjoining prayer for the sake of communication with God and not for the sake of displaying piety to be praised by men.

However, an ethic not dependent upon rules is not therefore an ethic without principles. The most antilegalistic book in the New Testament is undoubtedly Paul's letter to the Galatians. Yet even in the writing of that letter Paul foresaw the abuse to which it might be subjected. Hence he warned:

> "For you were called to freedom, brethren; only do not use your freedom as an opportunity for the flesh, but through love be servants of one another. For the whole law is fulfilled in one word, 'You shall love your neighbor as yourself.'" (Gal. 5:13-14.)

Paul goes on to recount a long list of prevalent vices and adds, "I warn you, as I warned you before, that those who do such things shall not inherit the kingdom of God" (v. 21). Then, as he describes the life of the Spirit, he says, "Bear one another's burdens, and so fulfil the law of Christ" (ch. 6:2).

"The law of Christ!" Then there is a law for the Christian, after all! Not a system of rules, with instructions for every situation, and not a system by which we can qualify to make demands on God. The Christian makes no claim of *meriting* any good thing from God. Yet an inclusive principle there is, indeed — the law of love. Jesus states it more fully, drawing on the Shema and universalizing an ancient Hebrew law regarding the treatment of Hebrews. In response to the question, "Which commandment is the first of all?"

> "Jesus answered, 'The first is, "Hear, O Israel: The Lord our God, the Lord is one; and you shall love the Lord your God with all your heart, and with all your soul, and with all your mind, and with all your strength." The second is this, "You shall love your neighbor as yourself."'" (Mark 12:28b-31. Cf. Deut. 6:4; Lev. 19:18; and Luke 10:25-27.)

Not only did Jesus restate the law of love and universalize it. He lived it in a way so profound and tragic and triumphant that he himself, even more than his words, became to his disciples "the law of Christ."

THE MEANING OF LOVE

On the centrality of love in the Christian life there is general agreement. When a definition of love is attempted, the agreement disappears and we are confronted with widely variant rival views.

The Augustinian doctrine that love (*caritas*) is the response to the lure of the divine is familiar to every student of church history. According to this view, obviously influenced by Augustine's Platonism, we love our neighbors because we see the divine in them, and when God loves us he is loving himself as reflected in us.[2] Besides the awkwardness of the doctrine that God's love is essentially self-love, this teaching fails to do justice to the love of the Christian for the ugliest sinner, which need not be a whit less than his love for the most godlike saint.

Bishop Joseph Butler set forth, in the eighteenth century, his doctrine of benevolence or general good will. For him Christian love was an active will to increase the well-being of all persons. Such good will would truly take us well beyond the level where most human life is lived. In his day Bishop Butler made a substantial contribution to Christian ethics. Yet his conception does not match New Testament teaching.

Even apart from the hedonistic assumptions that infected Bishop Butler's view, his interpretation does not do justice to the Biblical conception of love. It would take more than a general good will or disinterested benevolence to override the barriers of nation and class and to fashion into one body the ministering church of Christ. Moreover, we are called upon to love God. According to the Johannine writings, at least, we are to love him with the same love wherewith he loves us and we love our neighbors. To love God, in the sense of being actively concerned with promoting his well-being, would be quite impossible for one who understands the nature of God and of his relation to us in Biblical terms.

The idea of disinterested benevolence taught by Jonathan Edwards and prominent for a century in "the New England theology " includes more sense of God's transcendent holiness and a moving aesthetic reverence for being, yet suffers the same basic defects as Butler's view. If all men were actually motivated by disinterested benevolence, this would undoubtedly be a much different and better world. But this is not the revolutionary passion by which Christians have occasionally turned the world upside down. It does not even do justice to the cleansing power of the Great Awakening in which Edwards participated.

Undoubtedly, the most influential modern work on the meaning of Christian love is Anders Nygren's *Agape and Eros.* Nygren contrasts the seeking or aspiring love, *erōs,* with the giving love, *agapē,* and insists on their absolute separation. He recognizes that *erōs* can be a lofty, ennobling motive, reaching up for supreme truth, beauty, and goodness, even aspiring to the knowledge and likeness of God. But Christian love, *agapē,* he insists, has nothing in common with such striving for self-improvement, even in the best spiritual sense. The Christian, Nygren maintains, is called upon to love his neighbor with a giving love, unmixed with any aspiration to gain any kind of blessing — even the virtue of a loving spirit — for himself. Such love is quite impossible except as a gift of God. It is with such love that God loves us and he makes us gratefully to love our neighbors, regardless of their status or character.

Nygren has rendered the great service of recalling that Christian love is a reckless, passionate self-giving far removed from the prudent moderation of Butler's view and even outreaching the sublime serenity of Edwards'. However, there are grave objections to Nygren's interpretation.

The fact is that in the New Testament there is no such repudiation of aspiring love as Nygren's view would imply. Rather, there are many fervent exhortations to seek spiritual riches. Paul actually introduces his great discourse on love by exhorting the people of Corinth that they " earnestly desire the higher gifts," then adding, " And I will show you a still more excellent way " (I Cor. 12:31).

Are we, then, to aspire to various " higher gifts " one of which includes an absence of all aspiring? Is the " more excellent way " we are to seek a way that includes the renouncing of all desire for this or any other "excellent way"? Other objections also arise. We are commanded to love both God and neighbor with the same *agapē*. But how can we love God in the way described by Nygren as true *agapē*? We cannot pray to him in the hope of increasing his well-being and without hope of the relationship being of value to ourselves. To approach him with any spiritual aspiration, however, is, according to Nygren, to be at the level of the subchristian *erōs*. Hence Nygren insists that the command to "love" God does not really mean to love him. We are faithfully to obey him while loving our neighbors. But this doctrine does violence to the teaching of the Gospels and of I John.

Even in the loving of our neighbors, the superiority of *agapē* is highly questionable. Would you want your neighbor to love you in this way, desiring to serve you and do you good, but expecting nothing from the experience of worth to himself? It is to be doubted that this essentially aristocratic, condescending love is actually what is desired or needed.

All the views thus far canvassed, and especially Nygren's, fail at the same point to grasp one radical and all-important aspect of the *agapē* described in the New Testament. All assume a basically atomistic, individualistic society in which the most intimate relationship conceived is one in which an " I " confronts a " Thou."

The love described in John, ch. 17, in the First Letter of John, in I Cor., chs. 12 and 13, and in the whole book of The Acts goes far beyond such individualistic conceptions. The *agapē* of the New Testament is a *koinōnia* love. In *koinōnia* the " I " and " Thou " become " We," drawn together by the Holy Spirit and sharing " the unsearchable riches of Christ " (Eph. 3:8). In this profound fellowship (*koinōnia*), the individual self is surrendered, only to be regained and fulfilled in new depth and richness of meaning.

When we truly love anyone, even on a sub-Christian level, we seek to share with that person experiences that we prize. The ancient disciples of Christ possessed such a marvelous treasure in communion (*koinōnia*) with God, and in this treasure love was itself so important a part that they were fairly bursting with the desire to share this treasure with others. They did not desire only to pass on the treasure to others. They craved the intimate *sharing* of it with others — a very different matter.

This *koinōnia* love, this community in depth with God and with other human beings, is the love for lack of which people are dying in hopeless, barren loneliness. It is this which has been re-created by the Holy Spirit — in the monasteries of the Middle Ages, in the national Reformation revivals of the sixteenth and seventeenth centuries, in the United Societies formed by John Wesley, in some student work camps and cell groups of present times — whenever Christian faith has burst forth with new power in the world.

In the light of such *koinōnia* anyone should be able to see what is sub-Christian about ideals of *apartheid* or of " separate but equal " rights. It is good to send assistance to other people. It is useful to give for support of their churches and schools — as many racial separatists among the South African Afrikaners and among American Southern whites do on a scale that would put to shame the stinginess of many professed integrationists. But any amount of such giving still misses that Christian love without which all finally turns to ashes. For an essential aspect of all true Christian love is a craving to break down these artificial barriers that all may be one, even as the church described in I Cor., ch. 12, is one, and even as Christ and the Father are one. (See John, ch. 17.) Where true Christian faith rules men's hearts,

" there is neither Jew nor Greek, there is neither slave nor free, there is neither male nor female; for you are all one in Christ Jesus." (Gal. 3:23-28. Cf. Col. 3:5-11.)

It is for this sharing of the sacred treasure in intimate community that God's love created us. It is for this that he sought in Christ to reconcile us to himself. It is likewise for the sharing of this treasure in communion with him that we approach him in prayer. It is in gratitude for this communal love of God and in yearning for the extension of this meaning and joy that we reach out in evangelistic fervor, in sympathetic counsel, or in merciful healing to the lowliest, the most needy, and the vilest of men.

This is no mere loving in order to be loved, no prudent socializing mutuality. A desire for reciprocal friendship soon fails before the discouragements offered by the embittered lives that are actually neediest. Christian love, the *agapē* nurtured in *koinōnia,* is powerfully pushed forward by the surge of God's love already being received in the fellowship that has enfolded us. We cannot remain in that fellowship without seeking to extend it to even the most unlovely and hateful person whom we confront. Toward him this love expresses itself in any way that is open, but love's task is not complete until he too is so filled with God's love that he becomes one of the witnesses and ministers of its glory. If he never comes to this open receiving and giving, we can only continue to love him as we find opportunity, even when the sole opportunity left to us is intercessory prayer. For "love bears all things, believes all things, hopes all things, endures all things. Love never ends." (I Cor. 13:7-8.)

ASCETICISM AND SELF-REALIZATION

In New Testament ethics two recurrent themes are in polar tension. On the one hand, "I came that they may have life, and have it abundantly" (John 10:10). On the other hand, "If any man would come after me, let him deny himself and take up his cross and follow me" (Matt. 16:24).

It is common in recent years for theologians to attack all ethics of self-realization as Greek philosophical importations, contrary to the spirit of authentic Hebrew and Christian ways of thinking. There is certainly no doubt that the Greek philosophy of Plato and Aristotle was based on the belief that human beings should seek to realize in themselves and in other selves the *summum bonum.* Philosophical ethics through subsequent centuries has likewise been predominantly of this type. Some expressions of such concerns in the New Testament were probably influenced by Hellenic thought. After all, the New Testament was written in the Greek language and it would be quite absurd to suppose that Greek influence was wholly absent from it, even if we did not have such concrete positive evidence as we have.[3]

However, there is much evidence that the belief in self-realization was very deep-rooted in Hebrew religious life. The prophets, to be sure, often denounced luxurious living, pride in possessions, and eagerness to appropriate foreign culture. But such denunciation was based on belief that in the long run fullness of life, length of days, number of posterity, prosperity and peace, depended on faithful adherence to the nation's covenant with God. Consequently, all actions and interests contrary to the covenant must be rejected. Within the covenant the commands of God as given in the Old Testament often appear to constitute a nonteleological ethics of duty and to imply a basic asceticism. Actually, they are neither nonteleological nor basically ascetic. The purpose is always to gain all the rich blessings of the covenant.[4] This is made emphatically clear, again and again, in Deuteronomy. (E.g., see Deut. 5:33; 6:1-3, 10-25.)

In the New Testament, too, the purpose of accepting hardship, bearing a disciple's cross, and leaving all to follow Christ is often described as gaining the reward of God. Here the reward is not generally described in terms of long life, prosperity, and descendants. Rather, it is usually either an undefined blessing or reward (as in some Beatitudes of Matt. 5:3-12) or it is escape from condemnation and a place in the Kingdom of Heaven. In John it is "life," "eternal life," "light," "peace," or "joy." All these expressions are ways of promising the favor of God and all the blessings he seeks to share with those who love him. While in the Old Testament the rewards promised are usually for the nation, or, in the later prophets, for the faithful remnant, in the New Testament they are for individuals or for the people of the New Covenant.

The ethics of the New Testament, then, is thoroughly teleological, pointing always, explicitly or by implication, to the blessings of God's perfect reign. It is also an ethics of self-realization, not in the sense of assuming that a person is to be solely concerned with himself — and such an assumption would be foreign also to the ethics of Plato or Aristotle — but in the sense that the goals all concern the fulfillment of selves. Yet the New Testament plainly teaches that an individual's life is actually fulfilled or perfected in being given over to the service of God and his Kingdom.

It is highly significant that immediately after Jesus says, "If any man would come after me, let him deny himself and take up his cross and follow me," he continues, "For whoever would save his life will lose it, and whoever loses his life for my sake will find it" (Matt. 16:24-25).

Nevertheless, the crosses are real and the losing life must be thoroughgoing if the finding is to occur.

This is where our theologies often betray the gospel.

Liberal theology often accommodates to culture by easily identifying the ethical requirements of Jesus with the moral customs of the day, especially as far as individual, personal patterns of life are concerned.

The theologies that theoretically seek to restore the strenuous rigor of Jesus' ethics often actually remove it even more thoroughly. Interpreting all Jesus' commands in the most extreme sense possible, they show the utter impossibility of a society on earth in which there is no thinking about tomorrow, no refusal to give or lend, and no punishment but rather invariable reward for all who covet other people's property. Therefore the trick is not to obey Jesus' commands, but to " sin boldly," to be as " realistic " as the non-Christian, while always keeping the posture of " repentance " for this inevitably sinful life.

Conservative theology makes similar betrayals, the form of them depending on the particular tradition. Some conservatives simply minimize the importance of " works " to such an extent that all the weight of preaching and instruction falls on correctness of doctrine and above all on salvation by " faith." Sometimes the stress on faith is accompanied by promotion of certain actions such as the carrying of Bibles, the talking to everyone possible about the salvation of his soul, and the public saying of prayers. In some groups there is a teaching of radical nonconformity to culture in particular matters, often of trivial character. Thus women are forbidden to use cosmetics or young people are warned not to play cards or dance. In some conservative churches there is effective emphasis on personal kindness, honesty, sobriety, chastity, and generosity. So far there is real Christian challenge to the surrounding culture. However, while it is a challenge to many practices, it is not a challenge that provokes much real opposition — despite frequent conservative talk about being "persecuted for the Lord." Few people in our culture object to *other* people's being kind, honest, sober, chaste, and generous, even though they may prefer not to be so themselves and may prefer bibulous and sensual friends. In short, the real moral virtues most promoted by conservative churches at their best are virtues almost universally praised in our society at large.

On the other hand, as far as public social issues are concerned, theological conservatives in America usually ignore them or else side with the more wealthy, powerful, and socially conservative elements. While challenging some personal practices, our theological conservatives accommodate easily to the more powerful worldly forces in regard to the great social issues. Very little prophetic leadership has been given by the "Evangelicals" in dealing with racial discrimination, ruthless exploitation of natural resources for private gain, industrial strife, trampling on civil liberties by such men as Senator McCarthy, narrowly selfish nationalistic isolationism, or militaristic chauvinism. Indeed, often theologically conservative ministers have been among the most conspicuous attackers of all who raised a prophetic voice of protest against such evils.

There are some encouraging signs that the social conscience of conservatives is awaking. Some theological conservatives have joined in mild support of racial desegregation, and some recent fundamentalist revival meetings have been unsegregated. Carl F. H. Henry, Professor of Systematic Theology at Fuller Theological Seminary, and outstanding "Evangelical" leader, wrote *The Uneasy Conscience of Modern Fundamentalism* to lament the lack of social concern among conservatives. However, neither he nor his associates have yet taken a stand on any social issue that would lose them the support of many socially conservative men of wealth. The new magazine *Christianity Today* was founded to give voice to "Evangelical" Christian convictions on social issues. Neither its reported financial sponsorship nor its utterances thus far give evidence of more than the most timid departure from easy social accommodation. Yet it does give evidence that more serious study of social problems is beginning.

Curiously, then, liberal and neo-orthodox Christians in America tend increasingly to accommodate to the world in personal ethics though they challenge it on social issues, while conservative Christians usually accommodate on social issues, though some of them are nonconformists in personal practice. Neither position adequately represents Christian ethics.

There is something seriously wrong with our Christian discipleship when it easily accepts either the social condition of a world divided by artificial barriers of race, class, and nation, and filled with suspicion, fear, and hate, or, on the other hand, the sensuality, vulgarity, dishonesty, and materialistic hedonism that prevail in personal morals. Moreover, little will be done in either sphere by people who lack the courage and integrity to stand firm against personal self-indulgence while criticizing the policies of public officials, or to challenge the exploiters of other people's lives while seeking to purify their own. Too much that passes for prophetic courage is only easygoing conformity to the prejudices of the particular minorities of which we stand most in awe.

Christian asceticism goes deeper. It is a heeding of Christ's command, "You . . . must be perfect" (Matt. 5:48). It is the earnest, humble quest for the total sanctification of life in every sphere. Everything that obstructs the reign of God's will must go — whether it is wealth or friendship or peace of mind or life itself. On the other hand, to accept Christ and submit wholly to him is not to live a life of barren emptiness. It is true that "those who belong to Christ Jesus have crucified the flesh with its passions and desires" (Gal. 5:24). But it is also true that

> "the fruit of the Spirit is love, joy, peace, patience, kindness, goodness, faithfulness, gentleness, self-control; against such there is no law" (vs. 22-23).

All this and the sustaining love of God forever! What higher self-realization could there be?

LOVE AND JUSTICE

The supreme principle of Christian ethics is love. The most immediately relevant principle in many social situations is justice. True justice is the conduct immediately required by love where there are conflicting interests. In a realm of unlimited virtue, time, and resources of every kind, love would not need justice. In this world justice is required.

The attempt to express love without regard to justice results in wrongs that contradict the purposes of love.

When a convicted lawbreaker is before the judge for sentence, love uninformed by justice might seek to have him simply set free. Indeed, God may see his truly repentant and changed heart and say to him simply, "Go, and do not sin again" (cf. John 8:11). But the human judge does not know the heart so well. The crime may have been a fiendish attack on a young girl. The judge pronouncing sentence must, if he is Christian, love the wretched prisoner at the bar. He must also love all the families of the community, including other little girls and also including young men teetering uncertainly on the brink of similar crimes and needing only a little association with this fellow or even the encouragement of seeing him set free, to go over into the dark chasm. Justice, in the Christian sense, is the expression of love in this whole complex situation.

When the United States, with all its natural resources, military and political power, and responsibilities of leadership, faces an imperialistic, expansionist Soviet Union across the world, a Christian American citizen must determine his just course of action in relation to military preparedness. As a Christian he opposes everything that war is and means. To prepare for the mass destruction of human life or, what is worse, to require American youth so to prepare, violates every impulse of love for human beings, whether Americans or Russians. Yet in the light of recent history it may appear that to withdraw from Europe or Asia the protective threat of American air power armed with nuclear bombs would be to invite immediate war, with all its destructive fury, in Europe and Southeast Asia and elsewhere. If American pacifist sentiment should become strong enough seriously to weaken American military power and compel its withdrawal from foreign bases, it is certain that Soviet and Chinese arms would still not go unopposed and war would occur. Does Christian love seek to plunge the world into war? Does one prefer immediate actual war to continued preparation for war — perhaps with war in the end, but with the hope of averting that by other concurrent policies?

In confronting such problems the Christian must seek not only the way of love but the way of justice. Love requires a turning of the heart with gratitude to God and a generous yearning for true sharing of his grace with other persons. Justice requires also shrewd appraisal of forces in operation, of probable consequences to flow from alternative possible policies, and a wise weighing of prospective values and evils.

The attempt to have justice without love results in selfish pride, rationalized hate and cruelty, and the perpetuation of entrenched evil. The attempt to have love without careful and intelligent regard for justice results in sentimental indulgence toward persons in the focus of attention to the vast detriment of others and often the eventual defeat even of love's immediate object.

Justice and love are often described as in polar tension, or paradoxical opposition. Actually this is true only of unjust love and loveless justice. Thus, if it be assumed that justice in criminal law means the evenhanded application of a *lex talionis,* while love means only being kind to the prisoner at the bar, then the two are opposed. But retaliation, however evenhanded, is highly inadequate justice, while love requires concern for all and not only for the prisoner at the bar. To know what love requires is not an easy task for the presiding judge, nor is it easier to know justice. But justice and love are one.

This may be seen also in the economic sphere. What are the just wages to be paid the workers of a certain textile plant? If the owner-manager of this small plant is a true Christian, what does his Christian love require him to pay? In the end, do the two questions lead to different answers? In answering either, there must be considered the level of productivity, the competitive situation, the prospective demand, the condition of the plant, and the financial reserves. Will it be either wise loving or sound justice to put the wages so high that the product must be priced out of the market or the plant become decadent so that soon operations must stop and all the workers be thrown out of work? Will not both love and justice require that the long-range well-being of workers, consumers, and all affected by the policy be served in the best way that foresight, resourceful daring, and genuine interpersonal understanding can manage?

Is love, then, only another name for justice, or justice for love? No. Love is a dynamic intention. Justice is a right ordering of love's expression.

In confronting the complex social issues, we find in Christian love several contributions of the greatest significance.

First, love establishes the supreme goal — the community of grateful sharing in God's blessings. All action must be directed toward this end. We are to seek first his reign over all of life.

Secondly, love puts the agent himself in proper perspective. Without the love that God's grace elicits within us, we tend to measure the importance of everything by its effect on ourselves.

"Fifty people have been killed in a battle? . . . Where? . . . In eastern Algeria? . . . Oh, that's good. We don't know anybody there."

"A man has just been murdered by a convict? . . . Oh, the man killed was a convict too? Why weren't they in prison where such people belong? . . . Oh, they were in prison. Well, of course you can expect such things to happen among those people. What a blessing that we have prisons for them so they can't endanger society! . . . Yes, in a way the people in a prison are in society, too, I suppose. But you know what I mean."

The love of Christ changes all this. With Christ in the heart, we see the importance of everything by its relation to the reign of God in human life. Algerians and Frenchmen, too, are people. A murdered convict and his bitter killer are persons for whom Christ died.

Thirdly, love promotes resourceful daring. It does not settle down in comfort when even the most just sentence has been passed in the courtroom. Love seeks to improve the situation so fewer people will need to be arrested. In such seeking, love is willing to pay a great price. Without the constant renewal of love, justice protects the *status quo*. Love is never content with the present order. It does not take pleasure in putting the wicked in their place. Love rejoices only in good. So long as there remains one lost boy wandering in a far country, love yearns and seeks for his return to the Father's house. Love is willing even to die on a cross and so express supremely the justice of God in a sinful world.

Love is the creative, revolutionary forward edge of justice. Justice is the appropriate application of love in an imperfect and complex situation. Because our "knowledge is imperfect" our justice is always imperfect and will be superseded. But the Christian love that motivates justice at its best — this "love never ends" (I Cor. 13:8). Justice is at best a *modus vivendi* of the divine with the imperfect and the worldly. "Love is of God . . . for God is love." (I John 4:7-8.)

IX.

The Church and the Churches

REDISCOVERY OF THE CHURCH

In the mid-twentieth century there has been a remarkable revival of interest in the church, especially, but not solely, in America. The widespread new interest among Americans shows itself in rapidly expanding church membership, attendance, and support, as well as in many books and articles about the nature of the church. Some countries have not experienced the expanding participation in church life, but everywhere in Christendom there is new interest in doctrine concerning the nature of the church, its ministry, its authority, and its proper form of organization.

There are many influences that have given occasion for this rediscovery of the church.

In America some sociological conditions that have long drawn people away may now be pushing them back toward the church. For many years the increasing number of free associations of many kinds, recreational, fraternal, civic, and benevolent, together with the expansion of opportunities for entertainment, have competed with the attractions of the church and drawn many people away. Now, with the further vast expansion of facilities for entertainment, through television, automobiles, and pleasure boats, all these attractions have tended so to separate people into constantly changing groups that most acquaintances have become very superficial. When a person is with different people every day, excepting at work, where usually there is little chance for ripening friendship, he is likely to feel socially adrift as an individual. In many communities

153

the churches alone offer opportunity for many people to know one another in full family and personal relations at some degree of depth.

At the same time, the magnitude of problems that Americans face, with political freedom and even existence at stake, has produced intense anxieties and increasing search for trustworthy norms and spiritual security. Many are asking for the first time those ultimate questions about the meaning of life and death to which the Christian faith has immediate relevance.

Revival of religious concern is not necessarily identical with revival of participation in church life. Indeed, many people in Great Britain and America have long supposed that they could be as good Christians alone as in the churches. Was not religion a matter between a person and his God? What right had the church, then, to assume that it had a necessary part in the Christian life? While the ministers claimed that the church did have a necessary, or at least important, part in the Christian life, little serious thought had gone into the doctrinal interpretation of the nature and function of the church in the last two hundred years.

The new theological interest in the church is due in part to the discovery that individualism was inadequate. The passing of laissez-faire individualism in the economic order doubtless has been an important influence. At the same time, psychologists and sociologists have found many new evidences that we are to the very core of our being social in nature. No man is what he is, simply within his own individual life. He is what he is in his relations with other persons, real and imaginary, and in his own interpretation of his social role.

Again, the new theological interest in the church has been due to the rise of the ecumenical movement. In the various conferences of representatives from many churches, people from organizations without serious thought or tradition on the subject have encountered others who held clearly defined doctrines of the church. These doctrines are often highly annoying and repulsive to those who first confront them, but answer requires serious study and intellectual decision. Moreover, the attempt to worship together and especially to partake of the Lord's Supper together has raised problems about the church, in immediately practical, yet doctrinally searching, form. All efforts to move toward organic union of churches and many efforts even to co-operate have forced representatives to consider the church's understanding of itself.

All these influences have been heightened further by the great increase of interest in the whole range of theological problems.

BIBLICAL TEACHING ON CHURCH ORGANIZATION

It is doubtful that Jesus himself ever spoke of the church.[1] Yet he clearly made it inevitable. Calling a group of disciples around him, significantly a group of twelve, one for each tribe of Israel, he gave them remarkable instruction. They were to be "the salt of the earth" (Matt. 5:13), apparently an especially prepared remnant of the chosen people in whom the fulfillment of God's promises and purpose would be prepared. In Jesus the covenant of God with his people was renewed, and this new divine life among men was transmitted to them. (Cf. ch. 26:26-29.) They were to seek others to join them in repentance, renewed hope, and the glorification of God. All this was preparatory to the fulfillment of God's reign in power.

From this minimum of organization, it was inevitable that such a tremendous commission would lead to further organization as the company expanded. The book of The Acts, the Pauline epistles, and the pastoral epistles contain much evidence of such organizational growth. There are mentions of apostles, prophets, teachers, elders (or presbyters), deacons, and overseers (or bishops). We are told of certain requirements and duties of some of these offices. We read also the account of a general church council at Jerusalem, attended by "the apostles and the elders [presbyters]" (Acts 15:6).

There have occurred countless hours of debate concerning the proper organization of the church. Every Biblical reference to an elder (*presbyteros*), a deacon (*diakonos,* literally, "servant" or "helper"), or a bishop (*episkopos,* literally, "overseer") has been minutely analyzed and used to defend opposing doctrines concerning the nature, authority, and power of the ministry. Most of such discussion strikes the present writer as quite fruitless. The actual spirit of the New Testament churches, and also the spirit enjoined upon them, must receive our careful attention. (Cf. I Cor. 11:17-34, on the one hand, and I Cor. 12:4 to 14:1, on the other.) The form of organization is of historical interest, but little more. Between the primitive church and the churches of today there are vast differences of size, social situation, and the comparative educational and spiritual qualifications of leaders and lay members. To suppose that a bishop in the Roman Catholic, Anglican, or Methodist Church today should be assigned, or has been assigned, the power, authority, methods, or responsibilities of a New Testament *episkopos* just because there has been a historical evolution of the one office into the others is to lack historical perspective. It would be unrealistic to think that the form of organization that served the primitive church in the Corinth or Rome of the first century would necessarily be the form with which God would be most pleased in the New York or Accra of the twentieth.

As the Holy Spirit unites the people of Christ into one body, in a given place and time, they take on forms of organization relevant to the interaction between their spiritual purpose and the situation. It may be observed today that the organization of missionary churches formed by the Church of Scotland in Central Africa actually resembles more nearly the organization of churches formed by American Methodists or Congregationalists in the same region than it resembles the churches in Scotland or Presbyterian churches in America.

If we wish to learn how churches should be organized today and with what officers, we are not likely to get much help by studying the names and functions of church officials as they appear in the New Testament. The evidence is too sketchy, variable, and ambiguous, and the situation too radically different from our own. Even if we could find the clear outline of a single invariable form of church organization in the first century, it would by no means be proved that we should imitate it today. We might as well seek personally to imitate the clothing, diet, and daily schedule of Jesus.

There is constant need for us to renew effort to imitate the spirit of Jesus and also of the primitive church so far as the primitive church truly embodied his spirit. That is exactly the task from which we shrink in embarrassment. The effort to imitate the form in which that spirit was embodied is a frustrating and useless evasion of our Christian calling.

INVISIBLE CHURCH AND LIVING ECCLESIA

The New Testament speaks both of particular organized churches and also of that universal church of which Christ is the head. (Col. 1:18.)

This universal church has often been described as "the invisible church." As such it consists of all the persons known to God as saved by faith in Christ. It is invisible, not only in the literal sense, as being unseen by human eyes. It is not perceived in any way by men. It is beyond human experience and knowledge.

Does the New Testament ever speak of such an invisible church? Possibly, but no such teaching is ever made explicit, and it is never clearly implied.

On the other hand, there are indubitable references to a universal church. The words of Matt. 16:18 are probably not the words of Jesus himself. Yet they are clearly words that come to us out of the primitive church and affirm a faith concerning the foundation of the universal church and the Christ who is its builder.

Paul writes of this Christ who " is before all things " and in whom " all things hold together " [*synestēken:* "continue," or "are coherent "]:

> "He is the head of the body, the church; he is the beginning, the first-born from the dead, that in everything he might be preeminent." (Col. 1:18.)

What is this church of which Paul writes? Is it the invisible church? Is it the aggregate, unknown to man, of all persons saved by faith in Christ? The figure of "the body" would be a strange one to represent a mere aggregate. Such considerations have given rise to the notion of a kind of superpersonal church, having a life and mystical union of its own. Such a church, too, might be called the invisible church.

All notions of this kind break down before Paul's other statements about the church as " the body " of Christ. To be sure, some other passages would permit this same interpretation which would be allowed with some strain by Col. 1:18. (Cf. Col. 1:24; Eph. 1:23; 4:12; 5:30.) But not so the emphatic utterances in Romans and First Corinthians. There we find Paul making it quite explicit that the church is people, united in love, faith, and work. Thus he writes:

> " For as in one body we have many members, and all the members do not have the same function, so we, though many, are one body in Christ, and individually members one of another. . . . Love one another with brotherly affection. . . . Never flag in zeal. . . . Rejoice in your hope. . . . Live in harmony with one another." (Rom. 12:4-5, 10-12, 16.)

Similarly, pleading for more mutual consideration and love in the church at Corinth, Paul says forthrightly, " Now you are the body of Christ and individually members of it " (I Cor. 12:27).

What could be plainer? The body of Christ is not some mystical organism suspended above you, or somehow giving ontological status to orders, sacraments, and creeds. It is " you "! Among men and women on earth, " Where the Spirit of the Lord is, there is the one true Church, Apostolic and Universal." [2]

There remain difficulties. The members of the church are " members one of another " (Rom. 12:5) so that " if one member suffers, all suffer together; if one member is honored, all rejoice together " (I Cor. 12:26). In short, all are held in one fellowship (*koinōnia*) of Christian faith and love. Of whom is this true? Paul was writing specifically to

> " the church of God which is at Corinth, to those sanctified in Christ Jesus, called to be saints together with all those who in every place call on the name of our Lord Jesus Christ " (I Cor. 1:2).

He was writing especially to admonish, warn, and plead with the people at Corinth to heal their factional divisions and disputes. He addressed his letter, however, to include both the quarreling Christians of Corinth and also all other Christians everywhere! Apparently he knew that it was not only in Corinth that the church was not fully the church.

The condition of the church is much like that of a man. Often someone will say to a man, " Be a man! " This makes sense only because man is the one creature who must put forth an effort of will to be what he essentially is, and even then succeeds partially only by the help of God. Similarly, Paul is, in effect, writing to the church, at Corinth and everywhere, " Be the church! "

The true, essential nature of the church is in the purpose of God. He defined it before he created it through Christ, and the subsequent working of the Holy Spirit among men. The actually existing church only partially and fitfully realizes this essential nature. The existing church is partially a loose association of local clubs and institutes of many kinds.[3] Only partially is the church truly the church in the sense that distinguishes it as the church of Jesus Christ and not some other sort of association.

Nevertheless, at times there comes to the church, that is, to *us,* ourselves, the vivid, powerful experience of being the church, the body of Christ. When we are together at the Lord's Supper, or under the judgment of God conveyed in preaching, or in the silence of communal prayer, or in the devoted, Christian testimony of work together, we experience our unity in repentance, adoration, faith, and love, the love that is true *koinōnia.* So far as we are truly the church, we acknowledge in heart and life that Christ is our head and we are " members one of another."

Not some " invisible church " beyond our perception and knowledge, but this living church, this experienced, historic community of faith, is the true ecclesia, the body of Christ.[4] Neither its unity nor its apostolic authenticity can be guaranteed by the continuity of any series of ordinations, nor the verbal and ideational identity of creeds, nor the conformity of sacramental forms. All of these may be present without the unity of experiential faith and love that is the true *churchly* unity of the church. When the church is truly one, as church, it is not made one by bishops, words, or forms, but only by the grace of Christ to which human hearts, minds, and wills respond with faith.

Of this true ecclesia, alone, it is true that "outside the church there is no salvation." Of the true ecclesia this is true for two reasons. Only by the testimony of the living church in Scripture, work, teaching, preaching, prayer, and personal witness, have any of us been brought to faith in Christ. When we do accept Christ, we are impelled by the love of Christ in us to share in the fellowship of the ecclesia.

ORGANIZED CHURCHES

What is the connection between the ecclesia, the true, living church, and the organized churches?

Sometimes the connection is not close. The organized church may actually be hostile to the ecclesia. When the orders, forms, preferments, name, or statistics of the organization take priority over the universal fellowship of love and faith, the organization is in enmity to the true church. When ministers are kept so busy oiling the wheels of organization that they have little time for people or for God, the organization is becoming an idol.

This is not to minimize the importance of organization. The attempt to escape organization in order to gain spiritual effectiveness is vain. Church history in America abounds in futile protests against denominational machinery. A group of people determine to escape the divisiveness and preoccupations of denominations. They resolve to form a simple fellowship like that of the primitive church, eschewing organization, name, creed, and prescribed forms. On that day a new denomination is born, and before long it looks much like many another. Sometimes it is characterized by an extraordinary degree of pride and exclusiveness, vaunting itself as the true church and looking with condescension or contempt on "the denominations."

The organized church, whatever its age, size, orders, or traditions, is validated in its existence just so far as it is instrumentally useful to the living ecclesia. What promotes harmony and truth within the total fellowship of Christians and courageous, faithful, effective testimony for Christ by that fellowship to the world is good. Whatever hinders faith and the works of love is to be rejected.

Some ministers spend their lives in rebellion against the tasks of administration and all the other structured responsibilities of their work in the churches. Such rebellion is understandable, but it is futile. The need is for the breathing into administrative work such faith and love, expressed in such artful skills of organization, that administration itself becomes a means of grace.

The church organizations are not the church any more than church buildings are the church. They are necessary means by which the church lives in the world. There is only one thing required of them. They must be appropriate to the nature and mission of the church in the times and places where it is at work. There are advantages in some measure of continuity with church traditions so that the outer form may symbolize the continuity of the living ecclesia itself. But this formal continuity is no more than a symbol, and other considerations often outweigh the advantage of conveying traditional forms unchanged.

"Where the Spirit of the Lord is, there is the one true Church, Apostolic and Universal."

DIVISION AND UNITY

In the purpose of God the church is one. Unity is of its very essence, for the principle of its being is the *koinōnia* in Christ.

"There is one body and one Spirit, just as you were called to the one hope that belongs to your call, one Lord, one faith, one baptism, one God and Father of us all, who is above all and through all and in all." (Eph. 4:4-6.)

In this as in other respects, the church in its present existence is not true to its own nature. We look for the church and we find the churches. We long for the Christian fellowship transcending all barriers of race, nation, and class. We find churches claiming all kinds of theological justification for their separateness, but actually divided largely along the same lines as disrupt social relations in the world. If anyone doubts this, let him read *Social Sources of Denominationalism in America,* by H. Richard Niebuhr. There is much evidence to suggest that a similar thesis could be established in other lands.

There is much Christian fellowship that crosses denominational lines. In ecumenical discussions and work, from the World Council to local ministerial associations, people are sharing their testimonies of faith, are co-operating in certain tasks, and sometimes, on occasion, are worshiping together, despite their division into various organized churches.

The tragedy is that such ecumenical fellowship is limited principally to few persons, most of them at few times, and largely at superficial levels. Several large churches and many smaller ones refuse to participate, at some or all levels. Among those which do participate, most ministers and nearly all lay members are involved not at all or only slightly. Meanwhile, the regular fellowship of worship and church work, week by week, is within denominational boundaries.

Consequently, not only the organizational structure, but also the koinōnia which constitutes the life of the ecclesia, the body of Christ, is disrupted. Most of us are willing to concede that many churches besides our own are Christian churches and that many of their members are Christians. Yet our desire to draw near to them in Christian love does not overcome our desire to be separate, combined with the inertia of differing traditions and organizational structures. Our division is therefore both a consequence and a continuing cause of our failure truly to be the body of Christ.

Our failure is largely a failure of faith and love. It is partially a failure of knowledge and wisdom. We are not sure on what terms we have a right to unite. Certainly, a union that took us away from the Word which God has given us in Christ would not be an aid to the true ecclesia. As some churches now understand this Word, it is impossible for them to make any significant concession regarding doctrine or orders without betraying their callings. Yet all are convinced that the Lord is one and his people are rightly one.

There is no easy way out of this plight of the churches. The only way to genuine union is the way of drawing closer to Christ in heightened love and increased understanding of the truth.

It is encouraging that in our time the burden of the responsibility to seek such true union of the church has been laid upon many Christians, and that many are seeking earnestly to fulfill the calling of God to the end that all his people may be truly one.

When the churches have become fully what they were called to be, they will be one. "Where the Spirit of the Lord is, there is the one true Church, Apostolic and Universal."

X.

The End of All Things

FAITH AND ESCHATOLOGY

Every living faith has an eschatology. Only as men see by faith some goal that transcends present problems and struggles are they motivated to give life itself for significant changes in themselves and their surroundings.

The *eschata,* or "last things," to which various faiths point are not all *last* in the same sense. Marxian communism, for example, does not visualize an end of times in which physical sciences are employed to gain mastery over the world and expanded material comforts. It does hold out the promise of an end to the exploitation of labor, of class discriminations, of war, and of poverty. In the "classless socialist society" of the future the state will "wither away" and all people will live without fear or want. The theory of dialectical materialism assures such an outcome as the result of inexorable forces grounded in the material universe itself and exemplified in all human history. The Marxian eschatology has to do with the end, not of all things, but of capitalism and of the class struggle for peace and plenty.

Christian eschatology looks farther. No matter how the social structure may be changed, men will still die. While they live they will still ask whether death is the end or whether there is some life beyond death.

Christians do not share the utopian illusion of Marxism that changes in the economic and political structure will resolve all human frustration, hostility, and strife, and so fulfill all human need.

Now that Marxian ideology has for many years exercised unchallenged control over many millions of people, and is providing some material and educational advances long promised, the inevitable disillusionment is beginning. Dudintsev's book *Not by Bread Alone* comes like a cry out of the night, not the night of poverty, but the bleak darkness in which material goods are offered as substitute for the light of God.

Christian faith becomes relevant for persons who have asked ultimate questions about the end of life, a goal, however far off or near, sufficiently meaningful to redeem the costly travail of our present life and to fulfill the promise of our highest moments.

The Telos of the Christian Faith

When Jesus, as reported in the Synoptic Gospels, and Paul, as he writes in his letters, discuss the future, they do not customarily speak of "last things." No form of the word *eschata* appears in the Synoptic Gospels in an eschatological sense. There is only one such occurrence in the writings of Paul, namely, in the mention of "the last trumpet" in I Cor. 15:52. Those who assign II Timothy to Paul would find a second occurrence in II Tim. 3:1. Both Jesus and Paul speak repeatedly of the *telos,* or "end," especially "purposive end." In view of these facts, contemporary theologians would be more faithful to the New Testament revelation if they devoted more attention to teleology, the study of purposed ends, and less to eschatology, the study of last things. A *telos,* to be sure, may be a termination or conclusion. More characteristically, as well as by etymological relations, it implies a purposed goal, fulfillment, or consummation.

Thus, when it is written, "The end [*telos*] of all things is at hand," the author does not mean that the annihilation of all things is imminent. If he meant that, it would make no sense for him to continue as he does, "therefore keep sane and sober for your prayers" (I Peter 4:7). If some practical inference were to be drawn from the belief that all existence was about to cease, it might as well be concluded that one should eat, drink, and be merry, or that it would make no difference what one did. The end of which the epistle speaks is of a kind that heightens the significance of all that is done.

The Christian faith is characterized by the belief that there is no end in the sense of absolute termination. There is an end in the sense of goal. There is also a termination of this present existence, not a mere cessation but a consummation.

Since God is eternal and his Kingdom is forever, there could be no cessation of being. There is to be such a manifestation of his glory as will end the ambiguity and obscurity of our present existence.

It is this conception of the *telos* which provides the basis for the earnest Christian view of time and history. In the Orient, cyclical views of history predominate. Oriental views hold out hope of an end to the present cycle of trouble. But eventually the wheel will turn again and all must be repeated. Only the individual may escape this futile round. Hence the eschatology of the Oriental faiths is limited, and the social processes of human history become a barren repetition. Christian eschatology, on the other hand, is inclusively teleological. It provides both a personal and a social purpose of human existence. Both individual life and the historical process will be fulfilled in the Kingdom of God.

THE PRESENT REIGN OF GOD

The future reign of God is meaningful to us because to the eyes of faith his reign is already present.

In the Old Testament, especially in The Psalms, there are many acknowledgments of God's present reign. Sometimes his ruling majesty is seen in his ancient and never-ending sovereignty over his creation. Thus:

> " The Lord reigns; he is robed in majesty;
> the Lord is robed, he is girded with strength.
> Yes, the world is established; it shall never be moved;
> thy throne is established from of old;
> thou art from everlasting." (Ps. 93:1-2.)

This is, indeed, true. God reigns now. The causal laws discerned by the sciences are but aspects of his regular, orderly government.

In the affairs of the nations, too, God rules, and his judgments upon unrighteousness are terrible.

" The Lord reigns; let the people tremble!
  He sits enthroned upon the cherubim; let the earth quake! "
(Ps. 99:1.)

Such affirmation must rest more heavily upon faith. It is not always so evident that God's just reign is over the nations. The wicked and godless nation oppresses other peoples and boasts of its irresistible power. Peoples that seek freedom for themselves and for others, while harming or threatening no one, go under the iron heel of the oppressor. At such times it is not easy to see the judgments of God. In the long run of history, the oppressor too falls in frightful catastrophe. But that is small comfort to peoples now suffering and dying under his cruelty. Many of God's judgments can be seen in history. It requires the interpretation of faith to affirm that his judgment and not unrighteousness will have the last word.

While the judgment of God should strike fear to the hearts of all people, since all have sinned, more profoundly it is occasion for rejoicing:

" The Lord reigns; let the earth rejoice;
   let the many coastlands be glad! . . .
  Light dawns for the righteous,
   and joy for the upright in heart.
  Rejoice in the Lord, O you righteous,
   and give thanks to his holy name! " (Ps. 97:1, 11-12.)

Here the reader can see plainly that the psalmist is speaking both from experience and in anticipation of the future. What is thus far experienced is only a dawning of the day that is to be. This is precisely the situation of the Christian as well as of the ancient Hebrew. God's reign has been experienced and is experienced now. Yet it is veiled in ambiguity. The mists of night still obscure the light of dawn. The present fitful twilight is but the harbinger of the glorious day.

The Christian is living " between the times," as Karl Barth is so fond of saying. But Barth introduces a dangerous mistake when he minimizes the importance of all that we do here and now, so far as God's coming reign is concerned. Barth teaches that in Christ God has won the victory for us. At his coming again this victory will be made fully manifest. Meanwhile, evil, though doomed, goes on, like the pendulum of a clock swinging a few times after the mainspring has been broken, or a battle continuing in some remote area after the enemy has signed terms of surrender. All that we do now is under divine condemnation; yet we are justified in Christ. Nothing further that we can do will make any real difference in the long run.

Speaking of Barth's resultant " mood of eschatological irresponsibility," Reinhold Niebuhr writes truly:

" A neutralism having its geographical locus in little Switzerland and its theological locus in the knowledge of that 'big event' of Jesus Christ which makes all little events and changes of systems of small moment, is no longer informed by the Biblical impulse toward historical responsibilities. It has risen from the earth to a premature heaven, even though it calls that heaven the 'coming Kingdom of Christ.' Undiluted eschatology can be as irresponsible toward historic tasks as pure otherworldliness." [1]

Well said! Niebuhr rightly insists that we are responsible before God, even in the midst of all the ambiguity and perplexity of these times.

But so does Barth! The trouble is not that Barth denies Christian social responsibility here and now. He emphatically affirms such responsibility.[2] The trouble is that he has no principles by which to guide decision in regard to social problems and what we do has no direct and significant connection with the reign of God which, in any event, God will bring to full manifestation in his own good time. Since our acts do not affect the reign of God, what we are required to do has only arbitrary and unpredictable connection with the spirit and principles of that reign. It is small cause for wonder, then, that Barth seems unpredictable and historically irresponsible in his various oracular utterances on political, especially international, affairs.

The question must be raised whether Niebuhr has provided a sounder basis for moral judgment in such matters. In practice he has been more constant and predictable in political action than has Barth. But the connection between his political decisions and his

Christian theology is at times obscure, to say the least. For example, how did he move from his Christian commitment to his defense of the 1956 aggressive attack by Israel, France, and Great Britain upon Egypt? This is an illustration of the belief that Niebuhr shares with Barth — that "there is no moral answer to our moral dilemma," though "there is a religious answer," [3] the faith that in Christ we are justified. It may be suspected that Niebuhr actually draws his political direction from sources other than those presented in the structure of his present theology. The real sources may include his American patriotism, his long identification with the liberal wing of the Democratic Party, and vestiges of political thinking developed in his earlier days of liberal theology. It appears that the faith which he professes in these days would logically cut the ground from under any moral convictions that could train and direct any thoroughly earnest participation in world affairs here and now. For Niebuhr's faith is self-confessed as

> "a faith which knows that all our meanings for life and history are fulfilled *and refuted* by the final meaning that Christ gives to our private and collective destinies." [4]

To this, Biblical teaching would surely say "fulfilled," yes; but "refuted," no!

Niebuhr is helpful in warning against the belief that a simple, radical application of love, without regard to the complexities of our predicaments, will solve our social problems. He is correct in pointing out that such belief has led to some of the worst social policies.[5] But this does not imply, as he seems to think, that love is therefore irrelevant to our social problems. He is right when he says, "The Christian faith does not give us technical knowledge about the relations of our nation. . . ." It is imperative that maximum use be made of technical knowledge. But he underestimates the moral resources provided by the Christian faith when he says, "It can only inspire us to a sense of responsibility and justice . . ." It can also reprove our self-righteousness, incite our love, and remind us that any justice that is not motivated by love and directed toward the true goals of love is no justice.[6]

"Any form of the Christian faith which gives simple answers, involving the disavowal of responsibility for the sake of guaranteeing our own purity, is a part of the old liberal moralism . . ." [7]

This is true of liberal moralism at its insincere worst, though not of the great liberal theologians. I well remember my resentment when a pacifist inquired about my son who was defending a Marine outpost in Korea and then said smugly: "I am thankful that all the young men in our family are either ministers or conscientious objectors. We have nothing to do with the whole war business."

Such a person is, of course, self-deceived. Pacifism offers a dangerous temptation to just such self-deception besides involving a false analysis — and here again I agree with Niebuhr — of the probable consequences of pacifist decision. But self-righteousness does not characterize liberal theology any more than the moral passivity of some young Niebuhr enthusiasts who look condescendingly on all strenuous social action characterizes Niebuhr. The temptation to smug evasion is always with us, whatever our theology.

The thought on which I must insist is that the disavowal of "*simple* answers" to our social problems in the Christian faith does not imply the inference that there are *no* answers in the Christian faith. There are answers, but these answers must be applied to complex social situations with the utmost possible technical skill. Good intentions are not enough. Love without knowledge is not enough. On the other hand, knowledge without love is not enough. A loveless realism only compounds the disease. Hard-thinking, realistic, but forthright and daring expression of love is imperatively needed.

Even the best expression of love is never, in our complex social situation, fully satisfactory. Some of the predictable consequences of the most loving social action are such consequences as love regrets. Even Jesus foresaw that his own teaching and living of love would not "bring peace, but a sword," that it would "set a man against his father, and a daughter against her mother" (Matt. 10:34-35). So long as we live in a world where evil is rampant everywhere, even the purest expression of love possible will produce ambiguous results.

Does this mean that when "the final meaning that Christ gives to our private and collective destinies " is manifest in its fullness, the love of the historical Jesus and all the love of his most earnest and humble followers will be " refuted "? By no means. The best of our realistic knowledge and our clearest predictions of future consequences will be transcended, to be sure.

> " For our knowledge is imperfect and our prophecy is imperfect; but when the perfect comes, the imperfect will pass away. . . . Now I know in part; then I shall understand fully, even as I have been fully understood." (I Cor. 13:9, 12.)

On the other hand, " love never ends "; rather, " faith, hope, love abide, these three; but the greatest of these is love " (vs. 8, 13).

Is not love one of " our meanings for life and history "? It is if we are Christians. Is love finally refuted? By no means. It is perfected, cleansed of self-deception, of mistaken calculations, and of the ambiguous results that are inevitable in the present corrupted world. Love is perfected. Refuted? Never. It abides forever.

Christian eschatology promises fulfillment of our highest hopes which are informed by Christian ethics. The spirit represented by the Beatitudes, the whole Sermon on the Mount, the life of Jesus, and the many ethical teachings of Paul, is capable of being only ambiguously enacted in this present life, but even imperfectly realized it is in continuity with the spirit of the eternal Kingdom of God. Hence the most practical prayer of petition we can utter here, in this corrupt and perplexing life, is, " Thy kingdom come, thy will be done, on earth as it is in heaven."

The present reign of God over this world, however obscured to our perception, is the reign of the same divine purpose that is to be fulfilled in his glory. To obey his will here and now is to obey the same will which reigns to eternity.

LIFE AND DEATH

For all of us there is a veil drawn across the future. The name of this veil is death. However vigorously and clearly we project our plans to the years ahead, we always know that at some point unknown to us we shall cease to be participants in these plans. The curtain will soon be rung down on every individual life, and earth will know it no more.

As each life on earth ends in death, so at last the race of men will end in extinction. The day may be hastened by our suicidal cleverness in nuclear war. It may be postponed by devotion of our skills to overcoming the natural perils that threaten to overtake us. The time may be next year; it may be millions of years hence. But man's life is fragile and vulnerable. Among the physical conditions observable in the universe there is only a highly exacting combination that will sustain us. Among the heavenly bodies change and catastrophe are the rule. Our earthly existence as a race is doomed.

The experience of life frequently shows that Christians have no immunity to the suffering of gross injustice, pain, and early death. Righteousness makes for the good of all, but does not guarantee comfort, peace, or prosperity to its best exemplars. Both the Old Testament and New Testament frequently acknowledge this truth, and the cross emphasizes it. If in the end God's just love is to be vindicated, there must be, for individual persons and for the race, a life beyond death.

In recent conservative and neo-Reformation theology there have been many disavowals of the doctrine of immortality, as a pagan Greek, not a Christian, belief. Some of the neo-Reformation writers may be using such attacks as a protective device to cover their own disbelief in any life after death on any terms. Dismissing belief in immortality, they can insist on substituting the " Christian " doctrine of " the resurrection of the body." This sounds safely orthodox unless the attentive reader happens to notice that " the resurrection of the body " is taken as a " myth " or " symbol " and the precise meaning of it beyond the general belief in God's final triumph is left unstated. Often the reader who looks for some more exact statement is left in doubt whether such a writer actually believes in any life after death, on any terms.

There is a sound reason for theological objection to a doctrine of immortality if " immortality " is thought to imply an inherent imperishability of the human soul apart from God. But the word " immortality " (Greek, *athanasia*) has not traditionally carried such implication in Christian theology. Paul, as well as Plato, defended belief in immortality (*athanasia*), while the patristic description of the Lord's Supper as a "medicine of immortality" (*pharmakon athanasias*) shows especially clearly the repudiation of notions that immortality is inherent in the ontology of the soul. It is true that some of Plato's arguments in the *Phaedo* do imply an inherent immortality without any consideration of God. However, at least one of his arguments implies an immortality not inherent but gained through participation in the eternal Ideas.[8] However, Plato's arguments for immortality are rarely defended and are often rejected in modern philosophy. I can discover only one philosopher in the whole Occidental tradition who has defended a belief in human immortality apart from a belief in God, namely, J. E. M. McTaggart. He seems to have left no articulate converts to this doctrine. Philosophers who defend doctrines of immortality do so in the context of theism. Their hope of life after death rests upon their belief in the trustworthy power and goodness of God. Hence theological attacks on the philosophies of immortality apart from God are exercises in tilting at windmills. They exemplify one of many instances in which theologians display distorted understanding of modern philosophy in order to exaggerate the difference between philosophy and theology, to the disparagement of the former.

Another purpose in disavowing belief in immortality may be to declare the inadequacy of the notion that the human soul is to live, after death, in a disembodied state, with no means of communication. Anyone who wishes to protest such a view might do well to find it first in recent literature. That may not prove easy.

On the other hand, if it is intended to protest against the substitution of an eschatology limited to stress on a solely individual redemption to individual future life, in place of the historic Christian faith in the redeemed and everlasting community, then the protest is well founded. However, such individualistic notions of a future life are to be found chiefly, neither in philosophical nor in scholarly theological literature, but rather in popular conservative revivalism. Even there the social character of life in heaven would doubtless be accepted whenever the question was raised. The fault is not a *denial* of community in the future life, but an appeal to individual self-concern for individual salvation, simply neglecting the social involvements of our very being and distorting the Biblical doctrine of the redeemed society.

The Christian hope is the confidence that in God's purposive love and power as given to us in Jesus, we are restored to life after death, a life in company with God and all his people, glorious and eternal. With what body? Neither Paul nor any of us can answer directly, for we do not know. We can, like Paul, have confidence that God, who has made so many kinds of bodies, has power to provide for us in the future. The God whose love is so utterly given to us in Jesus can be relied upon to use this creative power for us hereafter.

If we were to take Paul's words very literally, we should infer from I Cor., ch. 15, that our present earthly bodies were themselves to be reconstituted in changed form suited to our future life. Yet even in that passage are some statements that might put Paul's intent in doubt. (Cf. especially vs. 39-42, and v. 50.) On the other hand, in II Cor., ch. 5, it is made quite explicit that this body is to be destroyed and we are to leave it, to " be away from the body and at home with the Lord " (v. 8). This does not mean that we are to be without any means of communication, as poor disembodied spirits. It is " not that we would be unclothed, but that we would be further clothed." [9]

Other questions crowd upon us. Are all human beings to live again after death or only those who are in the community of faith? What distinctions are there to be? Will all be saved eventually? How can people filled with the love of Christ ever enjoy the bliss of heaven if their sons or daughters, wives or husbands, or, indeed, any of God's children are shut out?

There is both ethical and Biblical ground for believing that God will grant to all persons renewed life of some kind after death. If he were to grant it to some and deny it to others, wherever the line were to be drawn, in terms of conduct or of faith, there would be a very minute difference between those who were accepted as barely worthy and the others who were rejected as unworthy of continued life. Yet for this minute difference an infinite distinction would be made between annihilation and everlasting life. There are New Testament teachings of life and death, light and darkness, and the like, especially in the Gospel of John, that could be interpreted in terms of conditional immortality. They are not explicit, however, and there is no necessity of such interpretation. There is much contrary expression, some of it quite explicit. Most of the New Testament and Christian tradition is well expressed in the words attributed to Jesus in the Fourth Gospel:

> "Do not marvel at this; for the hour is coming when *all* who are in the tombs will hear his voice and come forth, those who have done good, to the resurrection of life, and those who have done evil, to the resurrection of judgment." (John 5:28-29; emphasis mine.)

The New Testament, ethical considerations, and Christian tradition all agree in supporting the view that the *kind* of life to which we shall be raised will depend upon the character of our life here in this world. The doctrine of such distinctions is offensive only to sentimental suppositions that obedience to God's command does not matter much.

On the other hand, the common traditional supposition that those who do evil or who reject faith in Christ are to be consigned after this to an inescapable and never-ending punishment is offensive to all intelligent moral understanding and especially outrages disciplined Christian sensibilities. We marvel today that theologians of the Middle Ages could have taken unfeigned delight in picturing the tortures of the damned. Most recent theologians have either avoided the problem or sought in some way to refute or modify the doctrine of everlasting torment. Several, including Karl Barth and Emil Brunner, have found in the New Testament explicit assurance that at last all would be saved. Others, like Nels Ferré, have based such assurance on faith in God's love. At the least, it would seem that punishment after death must be regarded as administered in the *hope* and with the *purpose* of stirring the sinner from his complacent pride and preparing him for the redeeming work of God's love.

In any event, as Brunner rightly indicates, the Bible is mostly con-

cerned with our responsibility here and now. We ought here to seek
the redemption of the lost as if this life were all. It *is* all that we can
specifically plan, and willingly to put off a task until after death is
to disclaim our responsibility for it altogether. The traditional doctrine of the absolute and everlasting judgment has, then, a certain
practical justification, even if as a literal statement of God's purpose
for all eternity it is not true.[10]

Our main emphasis must continue to be on the hope that we have
in God the Father of our Lord Jesus Christ. All our hope is in him.
There is no other.

PROGRESS AND DISCONTINUITY

Much liberal preaching and teaching, especially among specialists
in religious education, has been preoccupied with the idea of gradual
progress. Properly defending patient, week-by-week instruction
against the notion that the Christian life is produced solely by a decision for Christ — usually in a revival campaign — many liberals
have unfortunately encouraged the notion of salvation by education
alone. In view of the popular American idea that the right kind of
education of youth can solve all social problems and attain all useful
goals, it has been easy to console ourselves, when most anxious and
perplexed, by the assurance that " it will take time." At best this may
be a good counsel of persistent hope, work, and faith. At worst —
and it is often at worst — the expected inference seems to be that
no one will need to do anything; the problems will solve themselves
if given time.

The fact is that problems do not solve themselves and time alone
solves nothing. Maturation helps with some personal problems; it
makes others more acute. Well-designed education can help much,
with many personal and social problems alike. There are serious
tasks that education cannot accomplish. Much less can they be done
by day-school formal education or church school education, compet-
ing for the mind and soul of youth against the most powerful emotional impact of vulgarity, brutality, and the appeal of quick, easy
money presented by television and other media of mass indoctrina-
tion. Moreover, advance is not always gradual. Both in individual

and in social life there are moments on which the future turns decisively. There is preparation for such moments. There are also necessary sequels if the effect is not to be lost. But no amount of gradual progress can take the place of decisive moments when the direction of development is resolutely reversed or the ideas of others become one's own secret of life.

The pathetic exclusive preoccupation of some conservatives with gaining initial decisions for Christ rightly stirs an eager counterconcern to gain continuing growth in the Christian life. Unfortunately, much effort is made to cultivate Christian living in persons who have not committed themselves to Christ at all. All the appeals of ministers, teachers, and friends concerning the "will of God," or the truly "Christian response," fall on the ears of people who have never decided to seek the will of God and do not much care what is the Christian response to the crises confronting them. In the lives of such persons the basic evangelistic work remains to be done. No amount of good ideas or good works will avail for them until they have made the essential commitment of themselves to Christ. This is not a matter of more gradual development. It is a matter of confrontation, of divine-human encounter, and of decision.

In the realm of nature there are many powerful gradual processes, like the changing of summer to winter in the temperate zones, the growing of a tree, and the reduction of a mountain by the erosion of wind, rain, and frost. But in nature is also the sudden bursting of a tropical deluge upon the parched earth to end the dry season and inaugurate "the rains." The tree that has grown for centuries may be split and scarred, or left a dead, charred hulk by the lightning that in a fraction of a second strikes from the sky and lights a conflagration in the forest. An island may be made in a day by a volcanic upheaval. A new star, a thousand times larger than the sun, may be lighted in one night, as a nova.

In the spiritual world, too, there are moments of sudden, cataclysmic change as well as years of preparation. Saul of Tarsus has been trained for years as a Pharisee of the Pharisees and with utmost fervor seeks to stamp out the rival movement of the Christians. Yet in one moment of time, on the road to Damascus, he is confronted by the risen Christ. Both Saul and the course of history are almost incredibly changed by that decisive moment.

When we consider the way in which the Kingdom of God is to come in its fullness, we must not overlook the possibility, indeed the probability, that there will be such sudden changes wrought by God as to offer challenge and opportunities now altogether beyond any human calculation. God has given us many surprises. It is likely that new events of great magnitude, with or without human participation, but impossible for us to anticipate, will yet occur, altering radically the very condition of subsequent human choices.

THE PAROUSIA

Some of the apocalyptic utterances attributed to Jesus in the Gospels point to such future events as we have been considering. Others of his statements, equally well attested, emphatically warn against apocalyptic expectations. As I have pointed out elsewhere,[11] neither the scholars who think Jesus was an apocalyptist nor those who believe he was not have a right to ignore the explicit and strong evidence opposing their views. On the whole, I have argued, there is more reason to think the records distorted in favor of the popular apocalypticism than in opposition to it. Albert Schweitzer's case for the belief that Jesus was a deluded apocalyptist is not nearly so strong as some readers have supposed. The weight of evidence favors the belief that Jesus saw the deluded and escapist character of the current apocalypticism and warned that the reign of God would come, not in a spectacular external display, but in the obedient faith of human hearts.[12]

Although, as they stand, the records are contradictory, the contradiction probably represents only a superficial misunderstanding, by the writers or their sources, of a deeper double-edged warning given by Jesus.

On the one hand, we are to live expectantly, knowing that God is at hand, and any day may bring such testing, opportunity, tragedy, and crisis of decision as we have never known. On the other hand, we are not to spend our time looking for signs and seeking to figure out how, where, and when God will act. The reign of God is not in its own essential nature an external affair. It is " within you " (Luke 17:21, American Standard Version), the ruling of your affections and will by the sovereign God. When we are at the end of our resources and see that all men are so, we are not to despair. God will yet act in our behalf. But this is a cause for faith, repentance, and loyal obedience, not for the dismissing of responsibility. Neither now nor ever shall we cease to be responsible to him.

The consummation of God's reign is often predicted in the New Testament as a coming again of Christ This need not be taken to mean a spectacular bodily descent of Jesus the Nazarene. The im agery used in the Gospels to describe the Parousia symbolizes mystery, and the divine majesty.[13] At the same time, the description of God's coming in power as a return of Christ implies confidence that his coming will be in character, as he is known in Jesus of Nazareth. He will not change, so as to show himself suddenly as a God of terrible vengeance as he is sometimes pictured in later Christian writings, especially during the persecutions. (Cf. Rev. 19:13-21.) Such a coming would belie the validity of his revelation in Jesus. No, God is the same, yesterday, today, and forever. His judgments are exacting and sinners tremble before him, but his purpose is love. The God who judges us is the God of Calvary.

This is highly significant. In the Parousia there will be no cancellation of the Word made flesh in Jesus. Eschatology is no excuse for moral irresponsibility or for attempts, like Reinhold Niebuhr's, to establish social responsibility without appeal to ultimate Christian principle. So far as we draw our guiding principles from Jesus of Nazareth, we are assured that " all our meanings for life and history are *fulfilled* . . . by the final meaning that Christ gives to our private and collective destinies." [14] Fulfilled, yes, fulfilled in pure, just love, without the ambiguities and obscurities of the most just expressions of love now possible for us in the present theater of action. Fulfilled, but not " refuted." [15] The same love that impels us now, as Christians, even in the most realistic and difficult weighing of ambiguous, alternative social policies, in search for the most just act of love, that love is to be fulfilled at last in unveiled splendor. Love abides.

What more can we say about the way in which the consummation is to come? How will the God who has come to us in Christ come again in complete manifestation of his glory?

In a limited sense, this may be a coming to us, one at a time, at the hour of our death. Jesus said to the repentant thief on the cross beside his own, " Truly, I say to you, today you will be with me in Paradise " (Luke 23:43). We may assume that in paradise the perfection of God's love is fully unveiled.

It must be observed that although this fulfillment at death comes to us one by one, it is nevertheless prepared in community and it is consummated in community. Jesus said, " with me." The thief's fellowship in faith was limited to his fellowship in dying with Jesus. Yet that comradeship with him was to be continued in the release and fulfillment of paradise. The communion of saints we can and do take with us. Indeed, without such communion there is no entering paradise.

What, then, of this great historical process upon earth? When and how is God's purpose for that to be fulfilled? Our constant prayer is that his Kingdom come and that his will be done " on earth as it is in heaven." However, in this world we can only hope that his will for us *in this world* will be done as perfectly as his will for heaven is done there. Limitations are built into earth that make the perfect fulfillment of his heavenly purpose for us impossible within the context of this mortal life.

The transition of death is continually shifting the scene of his purposive activity for us from this earth to the life beyond death. Since the whole of life on earth is masked with temporal limitation, just as surely the whole human episode on earth will one day end. All who have lived on earth will then be under the same Father's care and judgment and love in other realms beyond death. At that time he will have come to all his faithful children as he now comes to us and comes for us one by one.[16]

The important substantial center of Christian eschatology is that, despite all the alternations and uncertainties of this present life, God will have the last word and his last word will but fulfill his word of love spoken in Jesus Christ. It is precisely by that word of love that we Christians are bound now to guide our personal and social action, and in it we find the very meaning of "life and history." Because it is neither to be neglected now nor to be refuted hereafter, but will at last be fulfilled in sovereign glory, we can say, with Paul,

> "I am sure that neither death, nor life, nor angels, nor principalities, nor things present, nor things to come, nor powers, nor height, nor depth, nor anything else in all creation, will be able to separate us from the love of God in Christ Jesus our Lord" (Rom. 8:38-39).

The last things are of God, for God has the last word.

XI.

The Mission

ESSENTIAL TO CHRISTIAN FAITH ITSELF

To accept the gospel of Jesus Christ is to be in the church, since the church is a necessary means to the reception of the gospel, and also since participation in its life is essential to the very nature of Christian discipleship. To be in the church is to take part in the Christian world mission. These relationships are inherent and essential. When a person enters into the joy of Christian faith, he becomes part of a fellowship formed by the Holy Spirit and he enters the privilege and responsibility of a glorious new purpose given to that fellowship by him who formed it. That fellowship is the church and that purpose is the Christian world mission.

It is sometimes falsely supposed that a person who has accepted the gospel, committing himself by faith to Christian discipleship, may still look upon this as a purely personal decision. Whether he will subsequently choose membership in the living community of faith (*koinōnia; ekklēsia*) is for him an option loosely related to his saving Christian commitment. At the same time, persons who hold such views may think it quite natural and proper that only a minority of professing Christians share in the reponsibilities of the world mission. Consequently, many a person insists that he "can be just as good a Christian alone " as in church fellowship, and some local " churches " elect not to assume responsibilities for the world mission.

Such things could occur only where there is radical misunderstanding of the gospel, the church, and the mission. When these three are rightly understood, it is seen that to accept the gospel is to enter the church and to be involved in the mission. A " church " that is not participating in the world mission may be a useful organization in the community, with helpful teachings and social advantages. But to belong to such a local association does not make one a member of the ecclesia, the community of the New Covenant, the body of Christ concerning which we read in the New Testament. A church without participation in the world mission is a contradiction in terms. To be a church is to be an instrument of God in the world mission as well as to be a fruit of that mission.

The church exists as church only in the act of sharing its life, which it holds by faith and love, both among its members and among those who are not yet members. Its purpose is both to exist as the fruit of God's Spirit and also to be used as his instrument. The church is, as Wilhelm Andersen says, the " ' bridgehead ' of the Kingdom of God, which the Holy Spirit himself has brought into being in the world." [1] If a " church " is not eager to share its life beyond itself and beyond all barriers, then it is lacking in the very thing that constitutes a church, namely, the love given through Christ. For that love exists by giving itself boundlessly.

The Treasure Shared

Hendrik Kraemer says truly, " *Heilsgeschichte* has as its purpose the remanifestation of the unbroken (*heil,* whole) relationship of man with God, and of men with each other." [2] Hence Christian love is concerned with the whole of these relationships. Of course the ultimate and supreme objective of our mission must be to share our finest treasure, the reconciling love by which we are sent to our brothers. " In Christ God was reconciling the world to himself." (II Cor. 5:19, margin.) We must testify to this good news. But the testimony is given in many ways. When the love is genuine it includes the sharing of the lesser treasures of life also. Even in the sharing of medical skills, effective agricultural methods, and popular education, Christian love may be expressed. Indeed, love *must* be so expressed.

There are two great perils here against which the missionary needs to keep constant watch. Either the one or the other can be fatal to the effectiveness and even to the genuineness of the Christian mission.

On the one hand, there is the danger of being so preoccupied with the lesser treasures that "the pearl of great price" is forgotten or neglected. When this happens, the missionary becomes an emissary of "Western civilization" or of "enlightenment" and no longer a missionary of Christ. While sharing many things that are good he will fail to share what is best, without which all else will turn to dust and ashes. When we are true missionaries, "we are ambassadors for Christ, God making his appeal through us," and our appeal is this: "We beseech you on behalf of Christ, be reconciled to God" (II Cor. 5:20). The centrality of this appeal must not be lost, and about this there must be no equivocation.

On the other hand, there is danger of so "spiritualizing" the Christian mission as to cloak a selfish hypocrisy. We may say we are not sent to share Western wealth or techniques, but a greater treasure, our Christ. He is, indeed, greater beyond all comparison. But if we keep the advantages of industrial civilization for ourselves, while sharing Christ, there will be a well-founded suspicion that our "love" is an alloy of religious imperialism and material selfishness. In these days, many an African complains bitterly, "The white men have given us Bibles and taken our land." Those who say this suspect that the newcomers, despite their professions, cared more for the land than for the Bibles. It is small wonder that they are unconvinced when in some countries the people who now have most of the natural resources under their control talk of separating and so "protecting" the native African culture from foreign "contamination."

The same perils are a present danger in the homelands of our churches.

On the one hand, we may identify our mission in the world, as Christians, with efforts at social reform for the more equitable sharing of economic goods, economic opportunity, and political participation. In practice, however, this peril has never seriously threatened more than a small minority of people in the churches.

The other temptation is more inviting, easier, more comforting to our pride, and hence more dangerous. That is to identify the mission of the church simply with its "spiritual" task of preaching, teaching, administering the sacraments, prayer, and the pastoral ministry to individuals. Indeed, many laymen think that they "pay" to have these tasks done for them by the minister. Much as patients engage a doctor or litigants a lawyer, so Christians engage a minister whose duty it is to serve his clients (church members) and their families, and to keep up the roll so that the burden of support will not fall too heavily on a few.

Actually, every Christian is called to be a minister and a missionary. His own place of work is the place where primarily he discharges or fails to discharge his obligation as a Christian. The church building is the place where he receives guidance and inspiration, where he goes to hear the judgments of God, to receive forgiveness, and to be renewed for his own ministry during the week. Properly operating, as Protestants have historically understood it, the church accomplishes most of its work through its laymen, with its pastor serving as specialized leader and mediator of the Word to them, as they are its mediators to the world in every place where they live and work. "The priesthood of all believers" does not mean merely that every believer has immediate access to the throne of grace. It means also that every believer carries the responsibility for being a priest, minister, missionary, and evangelist to his neighbor. Some of this ministry may be accomplished by verbal testimony directly bearing witness for Christ in words. Much more of it is to be accomplished by doing the special work to which he is called in the spirit of Christ as a special ministry in his name. If God's will is to be done, as we pray, in business, in the home, on the farm, and in government, it will be done by dedicated, faithful businessmen, farmers, parents, and politicians.

If Christian love is truly in our hearts, we are bound to tell the good news of Christ. We shall do so by giving the "cup of cold water" in his name as well as by preaching and teaching. To render such ministry in every sphere, expressing love justly in all the tangled situations that confront us, requires much of knowledge and wisdom as well as loving purpose. The ministry is an exacting task, whether in pulpit of church or on bridge of ship, at altar or turret lathe, in church meeting or labor union meeting, in chapel or operating room. All these ministries are as important as they are difficult. The words without the deeds of love will soon be recognized as disclosing a hollow self-deception.

DEFENSE AND DEFENSIVENESS

When the Christian mission is carried on with vigor, in any land, it meets opposition of many kinds. None is more important than the intellectual opposition of contrary ideas.

Arguments against Christian faith are often raised by men and women who would seriously like to be Christians, but do not know how they can honestly accept the beliefs that they think Christian faith would imply. Such persons are especially numerous among college students. Often they have been reared in conservative homes where they have been taught that everything " the Bible says " is true. Now, after learning some facts of history, archaeology, and geology, they cannot honestly believe that only seventy-six generations separated Jesus, in the first century, from the first man to live on earth (cf. Luke 3:23-38); that pairs of all species of animal, bird, and reptile were taken on board one boat at one time (cf. Gen. 7:8-9, 15-16; 8:17); or that all the internal contradictions in the Bible regarding dates or sequences of events must be explained away, whereas similar contradictions in other ancient writings must be taken as signs of legend-making, guesswork, or inaccurate recording. Often similar problems arise in the minds of young people who have not been taught a doctrine of inerrant Scriptures by parents or ministers, but have, in early childhood, been taught a high respect for Biblical authority and have never been subsequently instructed regarding proper discrimination between authoritative and nonauthoritative aspects of the Bible. People who bring childish conceptions of religion to college are likely soon to feel the strain between infantile religion and the demands of critical maturity. Their religious ideas must rapidly mature, be discarded, or be put into a separate mental compartment, isolated from the daily business of scholarship.

Even young people who have been intelligently taught some critical discernment in their reading of the Bible may encounter grave difficulties. The whole temper of modern scientific scholarship produces in the student a demand for evidence as support for any belief offered for his acceptance. Many of his long-accepted notions of the physical universe, of human behavior, and of society are shattered by new evidence, and his whole conception of life becomes subject to review. The more complete is his sincerity, the more earnest his desire for truth, the more intense his concern to bring his religion into a substantial working relation with the rest of life, the more serious the intellectual crisis of religious doubt may become.

The college or university is one of the most important frontiers on which the Christian mission encounters non-Christian forces and ideas. How should their challenge be met?

The raising of this question brings us back to the problem of communication with which this book began. Communication is a two-way process. No instructor can teach very much, especially at the deeper levels of thought and evaluation, if he does not also listen to his students. Similarly, Christian faith cannot inform the interpretations of psychological, sociological, biological, and physical data unless theologians are willing to deal honestly with serious questions raised by the sciences and philosophy concerning their Christian faith.

To deal honestly with such questions is to be involved in the discipline long known as Christian apologetics. Our common connotation of the noun " apology " and the adjective " apologetic " makes this terminology unfortunate. Apologetics has nothing to do with an embarrassed expression of regret. It is a searching, rigorous study of the relations between Christian faith and the knowledge that we have from other quarters.

The influence of Karl Barth and Sören Kierkegaard, in our time, has challenged the propriety of Christian apologetics. Both Barth and Kierkegaard contend that to make an intellectual defense of Christianity is to betray it.[3] The only proper stance for the Christian, they say, is the affirmative, aggressive attitude of the prophet. There must be no defensive strategy, they insist, but only the constant offensive of proclaiming the gospel.

It seems to escape the notice of many people that the position of both Barth and Kierkegaard, relative to this matter, is a most desperately defensive one. It betrays the fear that in the open arena of intellectual search for truth, a Christian interpretation of life cannot stand. It leads to a religious isolationism. If this strategy is followed by Christians everywhere, the way will be left open for Marxian materialists, naturalistic humanists, and logical positivists to battle for control of contemporary philosophy and the basic assumptions and categories of the sciences, with Christian interpretations retiring from the scene without the firing of a shot. When, at last, anti-Christian Freudians and quasi behaviorists have completed the capture of psychology — including educational psychology — and humanists have taken over philosophy — including philosophy of education, philosophy of religion, and philosophy of law — Christianity will be reduced to the status of miserable existence in its own intellectual storm cave. From there it can emit only unreasoning pronouncements, becoming ever more irrelevant to the climate in which most people are being educated and governed.

The call for Christian apologetics is not a call for defensiveness. It is the call for an end of defensiveness and the seizing of the intellectual initiative. If we do not believe the Christian faith to be true in its basic assumptions, then we are not believers, and it is only a mockery to call ourselves Christians. If we do believe that the Christian faith is true in its basic assumptions, let us say so in every place where men and women are concerned with truth. If it is true in church, it is also true in the laboratory of science and the class in philosophy.

MAXIMUM INVOLVEMENT

Christians of strong and courageous faith are impatient with counsels of despair. The Christian mission requires that we set ourselves to the hard intellectual labor of showing the relation of psychological data to a Christian doctrine of man. We must relate the sociological data to a Christian doctrine of unchanging norms of righteousness grounded in the judgments of God, despite changing opinions and customs of men. We are called to show, in the light of arguments by the logical positivists, the necessity of living by a reasoned faith and not by faithless reason or by unreasoning credulity. It is our task to demonstrate in philosophy that the world can be seen in its wholeness of meaning and value only in the light of belief in a personal Ground of all being, the God who cares for the highest values in which we find life most meaningful and whole.

Such a strategy is dangerous to Christian faith, if this faith is founded on untruth. It is time to say, then, that if faith requires the acceptance of a falsehood, it ought to be not only endangered but destroyed. If it is true, its truth should be exhibited. Only those whose "faith" is already undermined and weak in conviction seek to insulate Christian doctrine from open examination. Such insulation is a defensive strategy, based on intellectual doubt or — especially among some young theological students — on intellectual laziness. Whatever its motivation, it is a counsel of despair and defeat.

When faith seeks to barricade itself against the threat of real two-way communication with the world, it is most in danger, because it betrays its own fearful doubt. A healthy, vigorous faith, firm in its conviction of truth and aggressive in its God-given mission to the world, accepts without fear the hazards of maximum involvement in the world's travail, thought, and toil.

God committed his purpose to the hazards of maximum involvement when he adopted the stratagem of the incarnation and the cross. Theology properly conceived must be similarly subjected to maximum involvement in the realm of thought. Such a discipline is Christian theology in liberal perspective.

Notes

INTRODUCTION

1. See Daniel Day Williams' chapter, "Niebuhr and Liberalism," Charles W. Kegley and Robert W. Bretall, editors, *Reinhold Niebuhr: His Religious, Social, and Political Thought*. The Macmillan Company, 1956.

2. Reinhold Niebuhr, essay on "Coherence, Incoherence, and Christian Faith," first published in *The Journal of Religion*, Vol. XXXI, No. 3, July, 1951, and republished in his book *Christian Realism and Political Problems*, pp. 189–190. Charles Scribner's Sons, 1953. All quotations from this book are used by permission of Charles Scribner's Sons.

3. See Walter Rauschenbusch, *A Theology for the Social Gospel* (The Macmillan Company, 1918), pp. 139–143, for his actual teaching on the divine origin and unique meaning of Christian love.

4. See Kegley and Bretall, *op. cit.*, pp. 196 and 441.

CHAPTER I.

1. The fact that the word "discover," in its various forms, seldom if ever occurs with its typical present meaning in familiar Biblical language is an accident of English development. In Elizabethan English, to "discover" meant (literally) to "uncover" or "disclose," not to "learn," by search or otherwise.

2. "*Qui ne s'appuie que sur l'expérience et la raison,*" Lalande, *Vocabulaire.*

3. James Hastings, *Encyclopaedia of Religion and Ethics.*

4. See F. R. Tennant, *Philosophical Theology*, Vol. II, pp. 78–120. The University Press, Cambridge, England, 1928–1930.

5. Further details, many other examples, and references to the

sources are to be found in E. H. Gillett, *God in Human Thought*. Scribner, Armstrong and Company, 1874.

6. Karl Barth, *The Knowledge of God and the Service of God*, tr. by J. L. M. Haire and Ian Henderson, p. 6. Charles Scribner's Sons, 1939.

7. *Ibid.*, p. 8.

8. *Ibid.*, p. 6.

9. *Ibid.*, p. 5.

10. *Ibid.*, p. 8.

11. *Ibid.*, pp. 8–9.

12. Karl Barth, *Church Dogmatics*, Vol. I, Pt. 1, *The Doctrine of the Word of God*, tr. by G. T. Thomson, pp. 448–449. Charles Scribner's Sons, 1936.

13. Barth, *The Knowledge of God and the Service of God*, p. 13.

14. Karl Barth, *Dogmatics in Outline*, tr. by G. T. Thomson, p. 38. Philosophical Library, Inc., 1949.

15. See e.g., Karl Barth, *Nein!* in *Natural Theology*, by Emil Brunner and Karl Barth, tr. by P. Fraenkel. Geoffrey Bles, Ltd.: The Centenary Press, London, 1946; *passim;* also Barth, *Dogmatics in Outline*, p. 17.

16. Cf. Walter Marshall Horton's comment on Protestant mediators, *Christian Theology: An Ecumenical Approach*, pp. 202–203. Harper & Brothers, 1955.

17. Barth, *The Knowledge of God and the Service of God*, pp. 8–9.

18. Note, for example, Calvin's citation of Cicero's natural theology in support of this teaching, in the *Institutes*, I. iii. 1.

19. Calvin, *Institutes*, IV. x. 5. Cf. IV. x. 16 and IV. x. 27.

20. *Ibid.*, I. iii. 1.

21. *Ibid.*, I. iv. 4.

22. *Ibid.*, I. iii. 1.

23. See John Wesley's *Notes on the New Testament*, 1775, Rom. 1:19; Rom. 2:14; " The Doctrine of Original Sin," 1757, *Works* (Jackson, editor), IX, p. 268; *ibid.*, pp. 268, 273. This is discussed instructively by Harald G. A. Lindström in *Wesley and Sanctification* (Stockholm, Nya Bokförlags Aktiebolaget, 1946), pp. 44–50.

24. Emil Brunner, *Revelation and Reason*, tr. by Olive Wyon, p. 62, n. The Westminster Press, 1946.

25. Barth, *The Knowledge of God and the Service of God*, pp. 13 and 18.

26. Barth, *Dogmatics in Outline*, p. 38.

27. *Ibid.,* p. 42.
28. Calvin, *Institutes,* I. iii. 1–3.
29. Barth, *The Knowledge of God and the Service of God,* pp. 6–7, 9.
30. *Ibid.,* p. 7.
31. Cf. definition above, p. 19.
32. Barth, *Kirchliche Dogmatik,* III, 4, p. 31.
33. See, e.g., *ibid.,* II, 2; III, 4. More is promised toward the end of IV.
34. See Introduction, note 2.
35. Niebuhr, *Christian Realism and Political Problems,* p. 175.
36. *Ibid.,* p. 177.
37. *Ibid.,* pp. 177–178.
38. Edgar S. Brightman, *Person and Reality,* p. 264. Posthumous publication, edited by Peter A. Bertocci *et al.* The Ronald Press Company, 1958.
39. Niebuhr, *Christian Realism and Political Problems,* p. 179.
40. *Ibid.,* p. 179.
41. *Ibid.*

CHAPTER II.

1. See, e.g., Ps. 109:6-19. Wesley's statement is in *The Sunday Service,* 1784.
2. Edward J. Carnell, *An Introduction to Christian Apologetics,* pp. 192–193. Wm. B. Eerdmans Publishing Company, 1948.
3. *Ibid.,* p. 193. Quoted from Edwin A. Burtt, *Types of Religious Philosophy,* p. 316.
4. Carnell, *An Introduction to Christian Apologetics,* p. 194.
5. *Ibid.,* p. 197.
6. Barth, *The Doctrine of the Word of God.*

CHAPTER III.

1. Used about thirty times in Matthew, fifteen in Mark, and twenty-five in Luke.
2. As in Jer. 49:18 and v. 33 (KJV). Cf. the many references to " the sons of men " in The Psalms.
3. As in Ezek. 2:1 and about ninety other passages.
4. E.g., see Justin Martyr, *First Apology,* Ch. 33.
5. Paul Tillich, *Systematic Theology,* Vol. II, pp. 101–107. The University of Chicago Press, 1957.
6. *Ibid.,* p. 107.
7. Of course we are speaking here, as is Tillich, of the epistemic

problems. Ontologically, the Christian regards both the evidence and the certitude of faith as gracious gifts of God.

8. Albert Schweitzer, *The Quest of the Historical Jesus*, p. 398. The Macmillan Company, 1950.

9. *Ibid.*, p. 399.

10. *Ibid.*

11. Tillich, *op. cit.*, p. 108.

12. Tillich is not to be charged with this offense, although he does not seem explicitly to regard the historic faith as a significant datum for historical research concerning Jesus of Nazareth. Rudolf Bultmann, on the other hand, does seem to regard as tenable the view here criticized. Cf. Bultmann's *Theology of the New Testament*, tr. by Kendrick Grobel, Vol. I, pp. 35–37, Charles Scribner's Sons, 1951. See also Barth, *The Doctrine of the Word of God*, p. 188.

13. Cf. Chapter X, below.

14. Schweitzer, *op. cit.*, p. 403.

15. Philip Schaff, *The Creeds of Christendom*, Vol. I, p. 21. Harper & Brothers, 1877.

16. *Ibid.*

17. *Ibid.*, pp. 27–28.

18. *Ibid.*, p. 28.

19. T. Herbert Bindley, *The Oecumenical Documents of the Faith*, 4th ed., revised by F. W. Green, pp. 234–235. Methuen & Co., Ltd., London, 1950.

20. *Ibid.*

21. Schweitzer, *op. cit.*, p. 403.

22. Contrast Sören Kierkegaard, *Philosophical Fragments*, p. 87. Princeton University Press, 1936.

23. Bindley, *op. cit.*, pp. 234–235.

24. Cf. Cyril C. Richardson, *The Doctrine of the Trinity*, pp. 31–35. Abingdon Press, 1958.

25. Cf. Sören Kierkegaard, *The Sickness Unto Death*.

26. William J. Wolf, *No Cross, No Crown*, p. 149. Doubleday & Co., Inc., 1957.

27. *Ibid.*, p. 120.

CHAPTER IV.

1. See Rudolf Otto, *The Idea of the Holy*. Oxford University Press, 1950.

2. See Thomas Aquinas, *Summa Theologica*, Part One, Question 2, Article 3.

3. The relation of the universe to God is in some ways analogous to the relation of a human body to the soul; but the serious limitations of such analogy make dubious the propriety of saying that "God has a body," as Nels F. S. Ferré affirms in his book *The Christian Understanding of God*, Harper & Brothers, 1951. In any event, Ferré's position would not essentially modify the above doctrine that God is completely free from any such body as ours.

4. See, e.g., the a fortiori argument of Matt. 7:9-11. Observe that in Jesus' parables God is always represented by a person: e.g., a father, a vineyard owner, a fisherman, a judge, a master of servants, or a farmer. Impersonal analogies could not convey the teachings given.

5. Cf. Henry Nelson Wieman's teaching that although God is not personal, we ought to pray and while praying to think of God as personal. See his book *The Source of Human Good* (University of Chicago Press, 1946), pp. 267–268. For philosophical evidence that God is personal, see Peter A. Bertocci, *The Empirical Argument for God in Late British Thought* (Harvard University Press, 1938); Charles Hartshorne, *Man's Vision of God and the Logic of Theism* (Willett, Clarke and Company, 1941); Edgar S. Brightman, *Person and Reality* (The Ronald Press Company, 1958); and F. R. Tennant, *Philosophical Theology* (The University Press, Cambridge, England, 1928–1930).

6. See Karl Heim, *The Transformation of the Scientific World View*, tr. by W. A. Whitehouse, Chapters 5 and 6. Harper & Brothers, 1953.

7. Alfred Tennyson, "The Higher Pantheism."

8. Richardson, *op. cit.*, p. 146.

9. *Ibid.*

10. Cf. Nicolas Berdyaev, *Slavery and Freedom* (Charles Scribner's Sons, 1944) and *The Destiny of Man* (Geoffrey Bles, Ltd.: The Centenary Press, London, 1945).

11. Richardson, *op. cit.*, p. 61.

12. *Ibid.*, p. 71.

13. *Ibid.*

CHAPTER V.

1. R. S. Franks, *The Doctrine of the Trinity*, p. 2. Gerald Duckworth and Company, Ltd., London, 1953.

2. E.g., cf. the Cappadocians of the fourth century and Leonard Hodgson, *The Doctrine of the Trinity* (James Nisbet & Co., Ltd., Lon-

don, 1943) in the twentieth century. For an acute criticism of Hodgson's view, see Claude Welch, *In This Name* (Charles Scribner's Sons, 1952), pp. 295–302.

3. Horton, *Christian Theology: An Ecumenical Approach*, p. 195.

4. *Ibid.*

5. Cf. Karl Barth's statement, ". . . something has been recorded in writing, namely, our life; and now a great stroke is drawn through the whole. It deserves to be stroked out and — thank God! — it will be stroked out." *Dogmatics in Outline*, p. 150. Barth has developed an increasingly affirmative attitude toward man in some of his later writings. Cf. Gerrit C. Berkouwer, *The Triumph of Grace in the Theology of Karl Barth*, tr. by Harry R. Boer (Wm. B. Eerdmans Publishing Company, 1956). Unfortunately, the influence of Barth's absolute deprecations of man, as that quoted above, continues, and much contemporary preaching and writing is in that negative mood.

6. Cf. Paul L. Holmer's article "Modern Theology — Another Evasion?" *The Christian Century*, Vol. LXXV, No. 4, January 22, 1958, pp. 101–103.

CHAPTER VI.

1. See Rauschenbusch, *A Theology for the Social Gospel*, pp. 57–90.

2. *Ibid.*, p. 58.

3. *Ibid.*, p. 61.

4. For further analyses see my book *A Theology of the Living Church* (Harper & Brothers, 1953), pp. 199–200.

5. Cf. Matt. 4:4. Cf. also the courageous and moving Russian novel *Not by Bread Alone*, by Vladimir Dudintsev, translated by Edith Bone (E. P. Dutton & Co., Inc., 1957), which has protested so searchingly against the barren materialism that is a logical outcome of Marxian ideology. I feel impelled to add two further observations on the book. It offers no solution, for without God the ideals that Dudintsev glorifies have neither ontological rootage nor ultimate triumph. The book should be disturbing to Americans, too, for Drozdovs and Avdiyevs are increasingly numerous and powerful in the bureaucracies of our own industries and government.

6. Paul Ramsey, *Basic Christian Ethics*, p. 255. Charles Scribner's Sons, 1950.

7. *Ibid.* Quoted from *The Confessions*, Bk. 13, Ch. 32.

8. Ramsey mistakenly attributes this doctrine of "'God' or 'perfection' in the neighbor" to Albert C. Knudson. Actually, in the passage

cited (Knudson, *Principles of Christian Ethics* [Abingdon Press, 1943],
pp. 130–131), Knudson is describing Augustine's view, not his own, and
he goes on to reject this view, for he always rejected notions of God as
being *in* man or man *in* God in the sense here implied.

9. Cf. Augustine, *The Confessions,* Bk. 1, Ch. 2; *ibid.,* Bk. 4, Ch. 12;
Bk. 10, Ch. 24; *On the Trinity,* Bk. 8, Ch. 8; Bk. 12, Ch. 4; *The City of
God,* Bk. 8, Chs. 8 and 9; *On Free Will,* Bk. 2, Chs. 12–15.

10. James 3:9. The Greek translated "in the likeness" here is *kath
homoiōsin,* quite unequivocally connoting resemblance or similarity.
Arndt and Gingrich regard this as a reference to Gen. 1:26; the Nestles,
as a reference to Gen. 1:27.

11. See I Cor. 2:11. Cf. also Augustine, *On the Trinity,* Bk. 15, Ch. 12;
and Bk. 10, Ch. 10.

CHAPTER VII.

1. Exceptions implying dedication or bringing into a relation to God
not explicitly conceived in moral terms include I Cor. 7:14 and John
17:19.

2. Wesley, "Working Out Our Own Salvation," 1788, *Works* (Jackson, editor), Vol. VI, p. 509. Quoted by Harald Lindström, *Wesley and
Sanctification,* p. 86, n. 5.

3. Calvin, *Institutes,* III. xiii. 5, last sentence.

4. *Ibid.,* III. xii. 8.

5. Of course Calvin believed that the preaching and the response
were alike predestined by the decrees of God. But we are not here concerned with Calvin's further dimension of explanation in terms of pre-
destination.

6. Cf. Chapter X, below.

7. Wesley, "The Scripture Way of Salvation," 1765, *Standard Sermons of John Wesley* (E. H. Sugden, editor), Vol. II, pp. 445–446.
Quoted by Harald Lindström in *Wesley and Sanctification,* p. 86.

8. Wesley, "Working Out Our Own Salvation," *loc. cit.*

9. Wesley, "The Scripture Way of Salvation," *loc. cit.*

10. See Lindström, *op. cit.,* pp. 140–154.

11. Holmer, "Modern Theology — Another Evasion?" p. 103.

12. *Ibid.*

13. *Ibid.,* p. 102.

CHAPTER VIII.

1. Luke 11:46. The phrase translated "lawyers" (*tois nomikois*)
does not imply quite the same kind of work as our word "lawyers." The

connotation is rather of *jurists* or *legal experts*. Of course the law referred to is the Jewish law.

2. Cf. Augustine, *On Christian Doctrine*, Bk. 1, Chs. 32, 33, 35. *On the Trinity*, Bk. 8, Ch. 8.

3. For learned discussion of Hellenistic influences in the thought of the New Testament, see the well-indexed volumes of Rudolf Bultmann, *The Theology of the New Testament* (Charles Scribner's Sons, Vol. I, 1951; Vol. II, 1955). Cf. Edwin Hatch, *The Influence of Greek Ideas and Usages Upon the Christian Church*, 1890 (Harper & Brothers, 1957).

4. Contrast the view stated by H. Richard Niebuhr in *Christian Ethics: Source of the Living Tradition* (edited with introductions by Waldo Beach and H. Richard Niebuhr, The Ronald Press Company, 1955), pp. 15–16.

CHAPTER IX.

1. Cf. my book *A Theology of the Living Church*, pp. 320–321. Harper & Brothers, 1953.

2. Second Affirmation of Faith, *The Methodist Hymnal*, p. 512. The Methodist Publishing House, 1939. These words introduce the exquisite creed prepared by Edwin Lewis, at the request of the Commission on Worship and Music, The Methodist Episcopal Church, and adopted by the Commission about 1934. See Herbert Welch, "The Story of a Creed," *The Christian Advocate*, Vol. 121, August 1, 1946, pp. 973 f.

3. The Roman Catholic Church even prides itself on its ambiguous character, for it claims that its papal government is the government of a state as well as of the church.

4. Cf. my book *A Theology of the Living Church*.

CHAPTER X.

1. Reinhold Niebuhr, "The Gospel in Future America," *The Christian Century*, Vol. LXXV, No. 25, June 18, 1958, p. 715.

2. E.g., see Karl Barth's little book, *Against the Stream*, Philosophical Library, Inc., 1954.

3. Niebuhr, *loc. cit.*

4. *Ibid*. Emphasis mine.

5. See especially Reinhold Niebuhr's book *The Irony of American History*, Charles Scribner's Sons, 1952.

6. Cf. the discussion of justice and love in Chapter VIII, above.

7. Niebuhr, *loc. cit.*

8. Of course it is not being argued that this is an idea satisfactory to Christian theology. It is aristocratic and unchristian.

9. More literally, " not that we wish to undress but to dress up! "

10. Cf. Emil Brunner, *Eternal Hope,* tr. by Harold Knight, pp. 179–184. The Westminster Press, 1954.

11. See *A Theology of the Living Church,* pp. 306–309.

12. Cf. *ibid.,* pp. 309–316.

13. See the analysis of this imagery in Paul S. Minear, *Christian Hope and the Second Coming* (The Westminster Press, 1954), especially Ch. 8.

14. Niebuhr, *loc. cit.* Cf. p. 169 above.

15. *Ibid.*

16. The possibility of interplanetary travel may suggest that in some future day colonies might be established on another planet. However, the same conditions of " change and decay " would still be confronted. Although the end of man as inhabitant of this physical universe might be thus postponed by space travel and transearthly colonization, the end would still come.

CHAPTER XI.

1. Wilhelm Andersen, *Toward a Theology of Mission,* p. 49. S.C.M. Press, Ltd., London, 1955.

2. Hendrik Kraemer, *The Communication of the Christian Faith,* p. 20. The Westminster Press, 1956.

3. Cf. Kierkegaard: " The Christian cause is in need of no *defense,* it is not served by any *defense* — it is *aggressive;* to defend it is of all misrepresentations the most inexcusable — it is *unconscious crafty treachery.*" *Christian Discourses,* p. 168. See also Barth's attacks on apologetics in *Credo* (Charles Scribner's Sons, 1936), pp. 185–186, and *The Doctrine of the Word of God,* p. 31.

Some Theological Books Written in Liberal Perspective

Baillie, Donald M., *God Was in Christ*. Charles Scribner's Sons, 1948.
Baillie, John, *Our Knowledge of God*. Charles Scribner's Sons, 1939.
—— *The Idea of Revelation in Recent Thought*. Columbia University Press, 1956.
Bennett, John C., *Christian Realism*. Charles Scribner's Sons, 1947.
Brown, William Adams, *Christian Theology in Outline*. Charles Scribner's Sons, 1906.
Calhoun, Robert L., *God and the Common Life*. Charles Scribner's Sons, 1935.
Casserley, J. V. Langmead, *Graceful Reason*. The Seabury Press, Inc., 1954.
Clarke, William N., *An Outline of Christian Theology*. Charles Scribner's Sons, 1908.
DeWolf, L. Harold, *The Religious Revolt Against Reason*. Harper & Brothers, 1949.
—— *A Theology of the Living Church*. Harper & Brothers, 1953.
—— *Trends and Frontiers of Religious Thought*. National Methodist Student Movement, 1955.
Harkness, Georgia E., *Christian Ethics*. Abingdon Press, 1957.
Horton, Walter M., *Christian Theology: An Ecumenical Approach*. Harper & Brothers, 1955.
Knudson, Albert C., *Basic Issues in Christian Thought*. Abingdon Press, 1950.
—— *The Doctrine of God*. Abingdon Press, 1930.
—— *The Doctrine of Redemption*. Abingdon Press, 1933.

—— *The Principles of Christian Ethics*. Abingdon Press, 1943.

Lewis, H. D., *Morals and the New Theology*. Harper & Brothers, 1948.

Murray, A. Victor, *Natural Religion and Christian Theology*. Harper & Brothers, 1956.

Pittenger, W. Norman, *Rethinking the Christian Message*. The Seabury Press, Inc., 1956.

Rall, Harris F., *Religion as Salvation*. Abingdon Press, 1953.

Raven, Charles E., *Natural Religion and Christian Theology*. Cambridge University Press, Cambridge, England, 1953.

Temple, William, *Nature, Man, and God*. Macmillan and Company, London, 1934.

Tennant, F. R., *Philosophical Theology*. 2 vols. Cambridge University Press, Cambridge, England, 1928–1930.

Thomas, George F., *Christian Ethics and Moral Philosophy*. Charles Scribner's Sons, 1955.

Williams, Daniel Day, *God's Grace and Man's Hope*. Harper & Brothers, 1949.

Index